# JAPANESE HISTORY

*Explore The Magnificent History, Culture, Mythology, Folklore, Wars, Legends, Great Achievements & More Of Japan*

HISTORY BROUGHT ALIVE

# FREE BONUS FROM HBA: EBOOK BUNDLE

Greetings!

First of all, thank you for reading our books. As fellow passionate readers of History and Mythology, we aim to create the very best books for our readers.

Now, we invite you to join our VIP list. As a welcome gift, we offer the History & Mythology Ebook Bundle below for free. Plus you can be the first to receive new books and exclusives! <u>Remember it's 100% free to join.</u>

Simply click the link below to join.

**<u>Keep up to date with us on:</u>**

YouTube: History Brought Alive

Facebook: History Brought Alive

www.historybroughtalive.com

# CONTENTS

# INTRODUCTION

Japan is a fascinating country with a long and storied history. While there are many books that explore Japan's unique history, few offer a complete and thorough explanation of this nation's history that is still readable and enjoyable. Many books try to do too much with too few pages. Oftentimes, important periods seem rushed or lack clarity. This unfortunately leaves the reader with a feeling of incompleteness. These books can also be hopelessly dry, overly academic, and just downright difficult to follow. Some authors even pad their books with unnecessary fluff and filler that serves only to distract from the juiciest details.

Fortunately, this isn't one of those books. This is History Brought Alive! In the pages that follow, you'll find tightly written and poignant information presented without bias. We strive to offer you a refreshing read with reliable, well-referenced information. This concise history will respect your time by getting right to the point and giving you the information, you came to learn.

We'll cover the most important parts of Japanese history, making this a must-have in your library. This book will serve as a reference guide for both scholars and history enthusiasts alike. We'll boil tens of thousands of years down to the essentials you need to know. After all, learning Japanese history ought to be enjoyable.

Why waste time with inferior books that will only confuse you and leave you with more questions than answers. Discover history the way it should be told, with History Brought Alive!

# CHAPTER 1
## *EARLY JAPAN*

J apan's storied history stretches back far before recorded history. The islands were a prime spot for early humans to find all manner of food and resources. There are some unique features that made this location ideal for early settlers.

Firstly, there are over 100 active volcanoes across Japan. This is about 10% of all the active volcanoes on the planet. This is due to the fact that Japan is situated upon the meeting point of two massive tectonic plates that form a horseshoe shape. This area is referred to as the Pacific Ring of Fire. It is known for earthquakes and volcanic activity which may sound like it would dissuade humans from visiting, much less settling there. However, there is a major benefit to living in a location like this. As we see in other volcanically formed archipelagos like Hawaii, the ash distributed by eruptions improved the fertility of the soil. Ash contains minerals that weather into the soil and nourish plants. Subsequently, a variety of edible plants for humans and animals alike flourished. The forests that grew here also provided a habitat for a variety of wild game which humans could hunt for food, hides, and other useful resources.

Secondly, Japan is an island chain. This provided natural protection from invasion as well as access to fishing in the bountiful seas surrounding the islands. Fish would become an important staple for Japan's earliest humans.

# The First People

## *Paleolithic People*

Some archeologists believe the history of human habitation of the Japanese archipelago could date back as far as 100,000 years. However, as with most of human history from long ago, there's not much in the way of tangible evidence. As we mentioned above, The Japanese archipelago would have made an attractive spot to early humans living on nearby islands or the mainland of Southeast Asia. So, it makes sense to assume human habitation of Japan goes back a long, long time.

The study of Paleolithic Japan relies heavily on stratigraphy or the study of soil layers. The volcanoes of Japan are quite helpful to archeologists since eruptions would cover the soil of the island with levels of volcanic ash which are easy to detect and useful as a reference for establishing dates.

The earliest human remains discovered in Japan were found in the Yamashita Caves in modern-day Okinawa. Archeologists found tools made of deer horns and bones along with the remains of a 7-year-old girl. Carbon dating revealed these to be around 32,000 years old, making them the first physical evidence we have of human habitation in the archipelago.

Around that time, there was an ice age which created lower sea levels. This in turn created land bridges that early settlers were able to walk across. One land bridge to the north connected the island of Sakhalin to Hokkaido. Another connected the Ryukyu Islands with Taiwan to the south. The lower sea levels also mean the Korea Strait was significantly narrower than it is today, making it another route ancient peoples may have used to reach Japan.

It is unclear whether or not the peoples who settled in Japan at this time are the ancestors of modern Japanese people. It is possible that they are, having assimilated with later groups that migrated here. It is equally likely that they died off and are not the ancestors of the modern Japanese.

Whether they are a part of the lineage of the modern-day Japanese or not, it is worth noting they were responsible for the creation of some of the first ground and polished stone tools in the world, dating back to around 30,000 BCE. In most of the rest of the world, comparable tools would not be seen until around 10,000 BCE.

The most prevalent theory is that the earliest

ancestors of modern Japanese people arrived in two waves of migration. The first migration is a group of people called the Jomon. The second group of people is known as the Yayoi. Let's take a look at them now.

## *The Jomon*

The Jomon Period spans from around 14,500 BCE to around 300 BCE. In the early Jomon Period, there are estimated to have been roughly 20,000 people living in the Japanese archipelago. They subsisted largely through hunting and gathering.

By the middle Jomon Periods, the population exploded to around 260,000 people. At this point, they had reached a high level of cultural complexity as evidenced by their elaborate tool making and jewelry made of stone, bone, and shells. They carved boats from tree trunks and used them for fishing and traveling, though it is unclear if they used sails or paddles.

Two of the biggest technological advances created by the Jomon People were the bow and arrow and pottery. These appear to have been invented independently by the Jomon People rather than being introduced from the outside.

Pottery was discovered as far back as the early Jomon Period. In fact, the word Jomon means "rope pattern." It refers to the unique and characteristic practice the Jomon people had of pressing rope or cord into wet clay before firing it to create a distinct textured appearance. This pottery allowed them to store food, water plants, and cook. It also allowed them to live further away from sources of water such as streams and rivers.

By the late Jomon, they had refined the longbow

to a point they could reliably fire arrows up to 50 to 60 meters away. However, due to the lack of stopping power these arrows had, historians believe they tipped their arrows with a poison such as a wolfsbane.

The Jomon People lived in round or rectangular houses with thatched roofs that were partially buried in the earth. These were known as "pit dwellings." They made use of indoor fireplaces for cooking and warmth.

It is a unique occurrence in history that the Jomon people were able to have such large and permanent dwellings without relying on agriculture. Typically, hunter-gatherers are nomadic people who follow the migration of animals they rely on for food. Scientists believe the fertile soil of Japan combined with warm, favorable weather conditions meant there was an abundance of nut-bearing trees and other food sources that made agriculture unnecessary.

As the population grew, larger and larger settlements formed. This gave birth to a network of trade between these different settlements. They were able to trade resources such as fish, meat, or certain varieties of edible plants. There was even a large village with over 700 buildings that appears to have been a central trade hub for the different villages. The Jomon Period appears to have been a time of relative peace. The skeletal remains found do not indicate a high incidence of death at the hands of other humans.

By the end of the Jomon Period, the population decreased sharply to only about 76,000. This massive depopulation was likely caused by food shortages. Since Jomon society relied heavily on Japan's abundant natural resources, this also made them susceptible to an adverse change in the climate. It is also likely that the increased population used their resources faster than nature could replenish them. Remember, they weren't farming on any appreciable scale, just taking the bounty of the earth and waiting for nature to give them more. This reduced population set the stage for the next wave of immigrants, the Yayoi.

## The Yayoi

The period from 300 BCE and 250 CE is known as the Yayoi period. Between 1,000 and 800 BCE, an ethnically distinct group of people known as the Yayoi migrated from the mainland to the Japanese archipelago. They mixed with the Jomon people to form the ancestors of the modern Japanese people.

One of the hallmarks of the Yayoi period is the shift from hunting and gathering towards agriculture. Compared to China and Europe,

Japan was very late to adopt farming. For context, here are a few things that were happening in the rest of the world at this time. Han Dynasty China was inventing paper, water clocks, and sundials, and the adjustable wrench. During this time, the Greek classical period was just ending. Greece had already advanced in philosophical thought, the art of theater, and a political system known as democracy. By the end of the Yayoi period, the mighty Roman Empire was in decline.

The origins of the Yayoi people are a matter of scholarly debate. Many historians suspect they came to Japan either via the Korean peninsula crossing the Tsushima Strait or from the north of China via the Yellow Sea.

When the Yayoi arrived, they encountered the Jomon people who had already been living on the Japanese archipelago for thousands of years. The Yayoi introduced them to techniques, such as wet-rice farming and metalworking.

One popular legend regarding the origins of the Yayoi people centers around a man named Xu Fu. As the story goes, China's first Emperor and Qin Dynasty founder, Qin Shi Huang, was the target of multiple assassination attempts. After the third attempt on his life, he grew obsessed with the idea of attaining immortality. He summoned his court sorcerer, Xu Fu. The emperor gave Xu Fu the task of finding an elixir of immortality. The emperor instructed Xu Fu to go find the mountain of the immortals where he would meet a thousand-year-old magician that would possess this potion. To this end, the emperor assembled a fleet of ships and recruited a crew of young men seeking adventure and honor.

Xu Fu returned after a few years and claimed

that a massive sea monster was obstructing their way. He requested the emperor equip his fleet with archers so they could slay the monster and proceed with their quest. The emperor granted his wish. Xu Fu and his fleet left the harbor, never to return. Legend says Xu Fu landed in Japan because he believed Mount Fuji was the fabled mountain of immortals. He and his men settled there and thus were the Yayoi people. It is improbable that this is more than a mere legend since there are some inconsistencies in matching up the timeline of the Yayoi's arrival in Japan and Xu Fu's voyage. Nevertheless, this tale does point to the importance of China's influence on Japan which we will see play out in the chapters to come.

Regardless of their origins, the Yayoi encountered a Jomon people that were in decline. They were hungry and had stripped the land of its resources. The Yayoi brought the technology of wet rice farming and changed everything. They set up rice paddies which provided a steady and reliable source of food to permanent settlements. This allowed for a massive population boom.

There is some debate among scholars as to whether the Yayoi peacefully assimilated the Jomon people or colonized them (*Origins of the Yayoi people*, 2008). What is clear is that there was cultural assimilation of Jomon practices such as living in pit dwellings. This indicates a high level of interaction and trade between the two groups.

Armed with their superior technology, the Yayoi population quickly outpaced the Jomon. They produced more simple, functional pottery than the Jomon. They created and popularized bronze bells and mirrors. They also developed spiritual practices that evolved over time into what would be known as the Shinto religion.

A major principle of the Yayoi belief system that would later develop into Shinto is the idea of purity (known as "harae"). Essentially, they posited that humans were born pure and collected impurity over time. Impurities (known as "kegare") included anything relating to death, childbirth, menstruation, and rape. These impurities could be cleansed from someone through rituals such as bathing. Such concepts and rituals persist in Japan to this day.

The growing ubiquity of wet rice farming introduced by the Yayoi meant that people stayed in permanent settlements. During this time, society also stratified into a strict class system. The growing inequality and importance of social class is still felt today in language and customs which aim to show respect from subordinates to their superiors. In Yayoi culture, men were able to have multiple wives.

Men of higher status had more wives than those of a lower social class.

The Yayoi did not have a writing system, so much of the information we have today about them comes from archeological evidence and the writings of the Chinese (*Prehistory of Japan (Paleolithic, Jōmon and Yayoi periods)*, n.d.). The Chinese record that during the time of the Yayoi, Japan was broken into 100 kingdoms. There were roughly 30 kingdoms that traded directly with Japan. With the growing inequality of social classes, those at the top amassed greater and greater wealth. This led to war and intense rivalries between the different kingdoms, powered by the newly introduced bronze weapons.

The Yayoi people lived in clans called "uji." The leader of each clan was not only a political leader, but also a religious leader of said clan.

Each clan had its own spirit (or god) called a "kami." When one clan conquered another, they also conquered its kami. This meant they grew in spiritual power. Eventually, one state emerged as the dominant force in Japan. This was known as the kingdom of Yamatai. Their ruler was a shaman-queen called Himiko. She partly achieved her power through trade as a tributary kingdom with China.

The influence of China on Japan in this period cannot be overstated. China was well aware of its political dominance throughout Asia. It asserted this power by forcing all kingdoms that traded with China to do so as a subservient, tributary state. These kingdoms would give gifts to China as a tribute to China's greatness. In return, China would give gifts, titles, and honors to these kingdoms. Japanese kingdoms that received this kind of recognition from mighty China gained a certain legitimacy in the region.

## *The Ainu*

To the north, lived another distinctly separate group of people from both the Yayoi and the Jomon People. While they may not have a lasting impact on the Jomon and Yayoi, their culture is unique, fascinating, and certainly deserves to be mentioned here. These people are known as the Ainu.

The Ainu inhabited Japan's northern island, Hokkaido. The majority of the estimated 25,000 remaining Ainu people living today still reside here. The origin of the Ainu people is largely unknown. Some claim they descended from a group of Jomon People who went north, breaking off from the main population and thus maintaining the hunter-gatherer lifestyle of Japan's early settlers. It is also possible that they came to Japan as a completely separate group of people.

The Ainu have a distinct appearance. They have light skin, European-shaped eyes, thick wavy hair, and the men grow full, thick beards. The Ainu women were covered in tattoos. This began as a small black dot on the upper lip. As they matured, more tattooing was added until a black tattoo surrounded the woman's mouth and eventually her forearms too. These were said to ward off evil spirits. The pain of tattooing was also supposed to prepare the woman for the pain of childbirth. In fact, a fully tattooed woman was a sign that she was of marrying age. Conversely, men never shaved past a certain age. Both men and women kept their hair at roughly shoulder length.

Like the mainland Japanese, the Ainu were animistic, meaning they believed that everything had a spirit (or "kami"). To the Ainu people, the chief amongst these was "Kim-un

Kamuy." This was the spirit of bears and the mountains. The bear was believed to be the highest god. The Ainu practiced a tradition known as "Iotame," which involved raising a bear from a cub as one of their children. Then, when the bear cub reached adulthood, the Ainu would sacrifice the bear to release the "kamuy."

The Ainu language was (and is) distinct from mainland Japanese. During the Meiji restoration in 1899, the Japanese government began a campaign of forced assimilation of the Ainu people. They outlawed the Ainu from speaking their native language or participating in their native customs. It was not until 1997 that this ban was lifted, though by this time Ainu culture had been all but wiped out. Today, the remaining Ainu are attempting to preserve their culture and pass it on to the next generations.

# CHAPTER 2
## *MYTHS*

Before moving further down the timeline of historical events, let's take a moment to talk about the colorful myths and legends of Japan. These tales and stories are as much a part of a society as its wars and migrations, perhaps even more so. To truly understand the Japanese people and culture, let's briefly examine some of the most popular myths that help shape the nation. We will, of course, be unable to recount every myth in the massive Japanese canon. We will also be unable to describe all the regional variations on each myth or the ways in which they changed over time. Here we will examine a few foundational myths that will help us to appreciate the culture of this rich and storied nation.

# The Japanese Creation Myth

Before there was land, the world was covered by an enormous sea. There were two kami (god or spirit) siblings named Izanagi and Izanami. These names translate literally into "he who invites" and "she who invites," respectively. They received orders from the other kami to solidify the shape of the Earth. Together, they thrust a jeweled spear into the water and churned it. Mud congealed on the tip of the spear. When they lifted the spear from the water, the mud fell into the sea forming an island.

Izanagi and Izanami went down to live on the island. They fell in love and married one another. They had eight children, which became the eight main islands of Japan. They gave birth to many more kami after that, such as the Kamis of wind, mountains, and rivers. When Izanami gave birth to the kami of fire, however, she was badly burned. Izanagi knelt beside his dying wife/sister in tears. As his tears fell, each tear created a new kami.

Izanami died and was sent to the underworld. In his grief, Izanagi went to the underworld to find her. Izanami told him that she would ask the kami of the underworld to release her but warned Izanagi not to look at her. After a time, curiosity got the better of Izanagi. He lit a torch so he could see his beloved Izanami once more. He was horrified to see that she was now a hideous, rotting corpse. In terror, he ran. Izanami chased him.

When Izanagi returned to the land of the living, he placed a giant boulder in front of the entrance to the underworld. From behind the boulder, Izanami yelled that she would kill 1,000 people every day if he left her. Izanagi replied that in that case, he could create 1,500 people every day. This explained why every day many people die and still more people are born.

Izanagi took a bath to purify himself. When Izanagi washed his left eye, the kami of the sun, Amaterasu, was created. When he washed his right eye, the kami of the moon, Tsukiyomi, was created. When he washed his nose, the kami of storms and the sea, Susanoo, was created. Amaterasu became the most important kami. All emperors of Japan claim to be descendants of this sun goddess.

# Amaterasu

Amaterasu is the powerful kami of the sun and one of the most important kami in Japanese mythology. As such, there are many myths about her. This is one of the most popular and enduring.

# Disappearance of the Sun

Susanoo, the kami of the seas, was neglecting his duties and cried about how he longed to see his mother, Izanami, in the underworld. So, his father, Izanagi, sent him to go live in the underworld. Prior to leaving, Susanoo decided to visit his sister, Amaterasu, to say goodbye. She knew of Susanoo's reputation as a troublemaker, so when she heard Susanoo was coming, she armed herself for battle. Susanoo was insulted that his sister did not trust him and they got into a big disagreement. To settle the argument, he challenged her to a contest. Amaterasu agreed.

Amaterasu asked for Susanoo's sword. She then broke it into three pieces. Then she chewed them up and spat them out, creating three new kami. Susanoo then asked Amaterasu for her jewels. He chewed them up and spit out five new kami. Susanoo won the contest.

Susanoo then began to gloat over his victory. In his raucous celebration, he destroyed farmland and property. He flayed a horse and threw it at Amaterasu's loom, inadvertently killing one of her maidens.

At this insult, Amaterasu went into a cave and shut herself in with a boulder. With the kami of the sun gone, the earth was plunged into darkness. Chaos ensued. The rest of the kami convened to see what they could do to convince Amaterasu to come out of the cave. They brought forth a large mirror. The kami Ame no

Uzume, The Great Persuader, danced naked before a cheering crowd.

Amaterasu peeked out from the cave to see why everyone was cheering and celebrating. Ame no Uzume told her an even better and more beautiful kami than Amaterasu had come. They held up the mirror, showing Amaterasu her reflection. Amaterasu pushed the boulder back further to get a better look when one of the kami pulled Amaterasu out from the cave. Another kami pushed the boulder back over the opening to the cave and sealed it shut with a sacred rope called "shimenawa," so she could not go back in.

Now that Amaterasu and her light returned to the world once again, the other kami approached Susanoo. As punishment for his behavior, they required him to provide 1,000 tables full of offerings to them. They shaved his beard, removed his nails, and cast him out of heaven.

## The Fabled Sword Kusanagi

At the coronation of each Japanese Emperor, they are presented with three items that serve as proof of the Emperor's divinity. These items are known as the Imperial Regalia. They consist of the jewel *Yasakani no Magatama* from the contest between Amaterasu and Susanoo mentioned above, the mirror *Yata no Kagami* that was used to lure Amaterasu from her cave in the previous myth, and the sword *Kusanagi no Tsurugi*.

This is the tale of how the kami Susanoo came to possess the sword Kusanagi.

Having been banished from heaven, Susanoo was walking beside a river when he came across two parents and their daughter who were all weeping. Susanoo asked them what was wrong. The parents told him that they had eight daughters, but every year a horrible serpent monster with eight heads, *Yamata no Orochi*, killed and ate one of their daughters. Now they had only one daughter left. They were crying because it was almost time for the serpent to arrive again and they feared they would lose their last remaining daughter.

Susanoo offered to slay the serpent in exchange for their daughter's hand in marriage. The family agreed. Susanoo turned the daughter into a comb. He puts the comb in his hair to keep the daughter safe and close by. Susanoo then instructed the old couple to fill eight vats with sake and place them behind a fence with eight gates, one behind each gate. The couple did as they were told.

When the serpent appeared, it fell for Susanoo's

trap and placed one head in each vat of sake to drink from it. Susanoo acted quickly, slicing off each of the eight heads one by one. Then he began to hack off the creature's tails as well. When he tried to slice off the forth tail, his sword broke. He discovered that inside this tail, there was an exquisite sword. He named the sword *Ame-no-Murakumo-no-Tsurugi* ("Heavenly Sword of Gathering Clouds). He presented this sword to Amaterasu to help make amends for his previous behavior towards her.

Many years later, under the reign of Emperor Keikō, the sword was given to Yamato Takeru, a great and powerful warrior. Takeru was lured into a grass field. His enemy used flaming arrows to set fire to the field, trapping Takeru, so he would die in the flames. Takeru used the sword to cut down the grass, so the fire could not spread. He discovered that the sword also had a magical ability to control the wind. He was able to use it to redirect the fire towards his enemies and win the battle. After this victory, Takeru renamed the sword *Kusanagi-no-Tsurugi* ("Grass Cutting Sword").

# CHAPTER 3
# *NARA AND HEIAN PERIODS*

## Nara Period

The Nara period lasted from 710 to 794 CE. This was the time when Japan's capital was in Heijo-kyo, or present-day Nara. This would become Japan's first permanent capital city. Prior to this, a new capital was built for each Japanese Emperor. This was likely due to the concept of impurity we mentioned in the previous chapter. The death of the Emperor made the old capital impure, therefore a new one needed to be built.

The capital at Nara was modeled after the Chinese capital and was the most lavish capital Japan had had thus far. The capital was moved a few times during the Nara period. In 740, Emperor Shōmu moved the capital to Kuni-kyo. In 743, it was moved to Shiragaki-kyo. Then in 745, the capital was moved back to Nara. Here it remained, until 784 when it was moved to Nagaoka-kyo. Then it was moved to Heian-kyo (modern day Kyoto) in 794.

The Nara period was the period in which the Fujiwara clan began their rise to power by marrying their daughters to Emperors and high-ranking officials in the Imperial Court. In 645 CE, Prince Nakano Ōe (later known as Emperor Tenji) had led a coup against the powerful Soga clan and seized power for himself. Nakatomi

Kamatari had assisted him in this coup. For his support, Emperor Tenji gave Nakatomi Kamatari the name Fujiwara.

A series of government reforms followed this coup that was known as the Taika No Kaishin, or Taika era reforms. As Japan moved towards a more powerful centralized government, a series of laws were put in place that made the position of the Emperor more and more influential.

During the Nara period, the Japanese also began writing. While there had been some writing during the prior Asuka period, it did not become widespread until the Nara period. It was in this period that the Nihon Shoki and Kojiki were written. These were a blend of history and myth that told the origin stories of Japan, Shinto legends, and solidified the legitimacy of the Japanese Emperors by claiming their direct descendants from the sun goddess, Amaterasu. The Nihon Shoki was written in Chinese, whereas the Kojiki was written in a blend of Chinese characters and unique Japanese characters.

This increase in writing would set the stage for an explosion of writing and innovation in the Heian Period that followed.

## Heian Period

Following the political reforms of the Nara Period, the Heian Period marks the era in which Japan's capital stayed in Heian-kyo (modern-day Kyoto). This period lasted from 794-1185 CE. While scholars disagree as to why exactly the capital was moved from Nara to Heian-kyo, a common theory posits that Emperor Kanmu wished to escape the political might of the Buddhist temples (*The Heian Period, an Age of Art... Ending in a Shogunate | History of Japan*

*34*, n.d.).

## *Why the Capital Moved to Heian-kyo*

In the late Nara Period, the retired Empress Kōken had fallen ill. She called for an ascetic monk by the name of Dōkyō. He claimed to have magical powers gained through his Buddhist spiritual practices which he used to cure the Empress. The Empress was grateful to Dōkyō and rewarded him by giving him titles and political power. There were rumors that the Empress even took Dōkyō as a lover. When the former Empress stripped Emperor Junnin of his rank and exiled him, she promoted Dōkyō to the position of daijō-daijin which gave him authority over religious and civil affairs. The Empress also instituted a new law that would allow her to pick her successor. Many assumed she would select Dōkyō. Since he did not have royal blood, this would end the old line of emperors and start a new line. There were also fears he would create a theocracy, giving

Buddhists political control over Japan.

Dōkyō promoted members of his relatively unknown and unprestigious clan to high-ranking government positions, including his brother. He limited the amount of land that nobles could own but set no such restrictions on Buddhist Temples.

The current nobles were understandably less than pleased with Dōkyō's rise to power, especially as it meant losing their own power. These tensions came to a head when an oracle delivered the prophecy that if Dōkyō were made Emperor, it would bring peace to the country. This enraged the nobles, particularly the Fujiwara clan. It was seen as confirmation of a coup by a lesser clan that would strip them of their power.

Shortly thereafter, in 770 CE, the Empress died. She had been Dōkyō's main champion. With her out of the picture, the Fujiwara clan moved quickly to strip Dōkyō of his rank and exile him. Dōkyō would die in relative obscurity.

It is likely the capital was moved to distance the Imperial court from a large number of Buddhist shrines in Nara. It is also possible that this incident, known as the Dōkyō Incident, was responsible for the lack of any female Emperors for the next 1,000 years.

## *Politics of Heian Japan*

At the start of the Heian Period, the Emperor had more power than ever before. Japan was much more unified than in the prior periods we've discussed. As always, Japan looked toward China for inspiration. The Chinese Emperor strove to be an absolute ruler (remember when we spoke in the previous chapter about the system of tributary trade China instituted). Early Heian emperors strove to attain this ideal.

However, in Japan, the political climate was different. People felt more loyalty to their clan than to the emperor. Thus, the top clans continually jockeyed for more political control. China used a civil service exam for government positions, meaning those who had proven their competence got promoted to higher ranks. In Japan, high-ranking positions were given based on clan loyalty and who they married.

In 781 CE, Kanmu was named emperor—the first of the Heian Period. In terms of his actual political authority, he was said to be the most powerful emperor in Japanese history. The Fujiwara clan had been the greatest threat to the authority of the emperor. But when Kanmu took the throne in 781 CE, there were no strong representatives of the clan in the imperial court.

Much of northern Japan was still not under Japanese imperial rule. Kanmu consequently sent armies to attack what were seen as the barbarian tribes that lived there. He also moved the capital twice: from Nara to Nagaoka-kyo, then to Heian-kyo. There was also a practice of giving shoen (tax-free, private land) to nobles as gifts, meaning there was less land being taxed. The combined effect of these changes was a massive drain on the government's financial resources.

To increase cash flow to the imperial coffers, Kanmu began to increase taxes on the provinces. He also set up two new important bureaus. The first was called the Kurodo-dokoro, which handled imperial documents. The other was called the Kebiishii, which was the Emperor's police force. The Kebiishii had the power to arrest, judge, and punish criminals (including tax evaders). These new bureaus consolidated power and allowed the emperor to eliminate half of the previous government offices. This also saved the government money.

Kanmu also began limiting the number of descendants that were considered a part of the imperial house. These royal family members were costly, as they were given riches, homes, and luxuries befitting of their station. Kanmu limited who was considered a member of the royal family. He limited this class to the fourth generation from the emperor. At the time he implemented this, it meant over 100 existing members of the imperial house were demoted. He also reduced the amount of money given to royal family members. Many of the demoted members left the capital and headed for the provinces. This inadvertently increased the political power of the provincial governments.

Due to a lack of funds, the imperial court also began paying court officials in land. Since this land could be used by the officials to make their own money, they became less reliant on the imperial court. The Emperor also claimed large tracts of land for himself, meaning there was even less taxable land.

All of these factors meant less power for the emperor and more power for the clans. Specifically, the Fujiwara clan. Since the clan had assisted Emperor Tenji to come to power back in the Nara Period, they had been able to leverage this to amass great power. This included a law that said Emperors had to marry either a Fujiwara or from the imperial family. Also, only Fujiwara men could marry the daughters of emperors. In 857, Fujiwara no Yoshifusa was named chancellor, which was the highest office besides emperor in the Japanese government.

The following year, Yoshifusa's son was named Emperor Seiwa. He was just nine years old at the time, making him Japan's first child emperor. He was also the first emperor to be controlled by a regent. Previously, the mothers of child emperors would take the throne until their son came of age, keeping the power in the hands of the royal family. The regent held the power of the emperor without having to be a member of the imperial family.

Then in 866 CE, one of the gates of the imperial palace burned down. It's unclear what the true cause of the fire was, but a court investigation placed the blame on the Otomo and Ki clans. These clans had held power in the imperial courts for generations and were some of the biggest obstacles to the Fujiwara dominance. By ousting them, the Fujiwara clan was able to step in and seize even more political control.

Now the Otomo and Ki clans were gone, Fujiwara no Yoshifusa had little trouble stepping into the role of regent. Yoshifusa's son, Fujiwara no Motosone, also became regent. In 884 CE, an adult emperor named Kōkō ascended. Since a regent could only rule for a child emperor, Motosone created the position of Kanpaku (regent for an adult emperor).

The office of Kanpaku became a permanent position that would remain in the control of the Fujiwara clan. This allowed them to maintain a stranglehold on the government for the next 200 years. At this point, the emperor of Japan lost all real political authority.

The upper classes had reached the pinnacle of what we might consider the "idle rich." This was an era when increasingly elaborate rituals became central to court life. The era came to be known for the "cult of beauty." It was fashionable for the upper classes to bemoan how fleeting all that is beautiful. This was likely influenced by the Buddhist idea that attachment to worldly things is the root of all suffering. However, suffering was also seen as quite fashionable.

## *Art and Romance*

Another distinguishing feature of the Heian Courts was what would be considered today as rampant cheating. There was a huge divide, of course, between the lives of upper-class aristocrats and the peasants of the provinces. Since surviving art and literature were generally created by the upper classes for the upper classes, it's this small section of society we have the clearest understanding of—it was fascinating.

In the Heian era, court ladies had more freedom

than in previous eras, yet they could not leave their homes, except on special occasions such as festivals or to visit temples. Women at this time were paradoxically considered inferior to men and, at the same time, more valuable than men. The teachings of the Chinese philosopher Confucius emphasized that women were inferior. Buddhist teachings claimed that a woman had to be reincarnated as a man before they could attain enlightenment. Women could not take part in government. However, inheritance of property generally went to women, violence against women was prohibited, and, due to marriage politics, women were able to climb the social ladder through marriage more easily than men.

Women mostly remained in their private quarters, greeting visitors only when hidden behind screens. Most of their communication was done via exchanging notes, which contained poetry. Being able to compose beautiful poems on the spot was an important skill that was expected of all nobles of this time period.

Noblewomen were also not allowed to do their own housework, or even to raise their own children. Much of their lives consisted of idle time and boredom. Common hobbies of the time included practicing arts, such as music and calligraphy. The board game *Go* was also a popular pastime.

Another common pastime for Heian women was writing. While men of the era were expected to learn Chinese and write for practical, business-related purposes, women were free to experiment. It was at this time that the new Japanese script Hiragana, meaning simple script (simple as opposed to Chinese characters known as kanji). Interestingly, famous authors of this era were almost all women.

This was the time in which Sei Shōnagon wrote her famous collection of musings on courtly life known as *The Pillow Book*. Another author named Murasaki Shikibu wrote a book that is widely considered to be the first modern novel, *The Tale of Genji*. Shikibu's story was among the first to focus on the inner emotional lives of its characters rather than place focus on a recitation of events. The book tells the story of Genji, a fictional son of a fictional emperor, and the tragedies of his many romantic conquests.

Though fictional, *The Tale of Genji* provides insight into the intrigue of court life. Cheating was an open secret amongst the upper class. A man was expected to take many lovers. Women were supposed to remain faithful to their men, however, in practice, this just meant to not get caught cheating.

There were no strong religious ideas about sex

being sinful, like in Judeo-Christian traditions. There was a custom that men would exchange letters and poems with the woman he desired. If she showed interest in return, he would sneak into her house and attempt to woo and seduce her. A man of the high station was expected to have many mistresses. Marriages past the first marriage were not an official legal process either. If a man continued to see a woman, they could be said to be married. If he stopped seeing her, that could be considered a divorce. But if he came back later, he may say that he never divorced her. So relationships could get a bit complicated.

Women of the Heian era also had a very distinct sense of fashion. They wore stark white makeup, drew their eyebrows high on their forehead, and stained their teeth black. They wore layers of robes in a style known as *ni-hito* (literally meaning "12 layers"), though some women wore as many as 40 layers depending on their status and the occasion.

## The Genpei War

This quiet, peaceful time of poetry appreciation couldn't last forever, though. In fact, it ended with a bloody civil war that began the era of samurai rule in Japan. This civil war was known as the Genpei War.

The major players in the conflict were the Taira and Minamoto, clans. The two clans had been vying for control of the Imperial court for decades. During the Hōgen and Heiji Rebellions, the Minamoto clan attempted to take control of the Taira clan but were unsuccessful.

In 1180, Emperor Takakura abdicated. Taira no Kiyomori put his two-year-old grandson on the throne. Mochihito, the son of Emperor Go-

Shirakawa, was furious. He felt he had been denied his right to the throne. Jumping at the chance to take down the Taira, Minamoto no Yorimasa mobilized the Minamoto clan and sought help from Buddhist monasteries.

Kiyomori called for Mochihito's arrest. The Taira chased Mochihito to Byōdō-in, just outside the capital. The forces met at the bridge over the river Uji in the first dramatic battle of the war. The Taira overpowered the Minamoto forces. Yorimasa committed *seppuku*, an honorable suicide of the feudal Japanese samurai class, and Mochihito was executed.

Enraged by their loss, Minamoto's new leader, Minamoto no Yoritomo, began calling for allied clans to join his side and fight the Taira. On his travels, Yoritomo and his forces were repelled by the Taira at Hakone Pass. The Minamoto found supporters in the provinces of Kōzuke and Kai who helped them to fend off the Taira.

Then in 1181 CE, Taira no Kiyomori died of fever. A famine followed and the fighting stopped for two years. When the fighting resumed with the Battle of Kurikara in 1183, the Taira suffered a devastating defeat. The Minamoto forced the Taira army to flee the capital.

The years following saw the Taira fighting vainly to reassert their control and find a foothold. At last, in 1185 CE, the war culminated in a great sea battle called the Battle of Dan-no-ura. The Minamoto defeated the Taira and brought an end to Taira dominance in the Imperial courts once and for all. Emperor Go-Shirakawa gave Minamoto no Yoritomo the power to collect taxes and appoint *jito* (stewards) and *shugo* (constables) in all of the provinces. This meant the emperor had just handed over all real political power to a military leader. When Emperor Go-Shirakawa died in 1192 CE, Yoritomo was given the title of *Sei-i Tai Shōgun* (literally "barbarian-subduing great general"). The seat of the shogunate, Kamakura, was now the effective capital. Kyoto was relegated to a place of ceremony and ritual.

The age of the samurai was about to begin.

# CHAPTER 4
## *KAMAKURA PERIOD*

The Kamakura Period lasted from the end of the Genpei War in 1185 CE until the violent end of the Kamakura shogunate in 1333 CE. It was the time in which the samurai came to power and feudalism was established in Japan.

Minamoto no Yoritomo, now the leader of the new military government, set to work murdering his potential rivals—starting with his brother Yoshitsune. He went on to kill his nephew, the son Yoshitsune had by a concubine. He also killed another one of his brothers, Noriyori, and his daughter's fiance.

While Yoritomo's new shogunate in Kamakura held all the military power, he still made sure to get official authorization from the Kyoto government for all his policies. When Yoritomo died in 1199, the title of shogun passed to his son, Yoriie.

Yoritomo's wife, Hojo Masako, had strong loyalty to the Hojo clan, which was a small part of the larger Taira clan. Her father was Hojo Tokimasa, head of the Hojo family and lord of some lands in the Izu province. There is an interesting story surrounding the way Masako and Yoritomo met. After his father had been defeated by the Taira during the Heiji Rebellion, Yoritomo had been banished to the Izu province. During his exile, Masako's sister caught his eye. So he wrote a letter and asked a samurai to deliver it to her. But the samurai delivered the letter to Masako by mistake. Her father, Tokimasa, understandably disapproved of his daughter marrying a Minamoto and forbade Masako from marrying him. In defiance, Masako ran away from home in the night, embarking on a long mountain trek to be with Yoritomo. The two lived in hiding in a mountain temple until Tokimasa at last relented and allowed them to marry.

The Hojo did not want Yoriie to be shogun. The Hojo placed Yoriie under house arrest for plotting against the Hojo. Yoriie was assassinated by the clan a year later. The title of shogun then passed to his younger brother, Sanetomo. He was just a child at the time, meaning he would need a regent to rule for him. This made the shogun a mere figurehead, while the Hojo regents held all the real power—an arrangement that would last through the end of the Kamakura Period.

After Yoritomo's death, Hojo Masako became a nun. But despite her religious vows, she went about amassing more political power. Thus, she would be known as the Nun Shogun.

## Jokyu War

Retired Emperor Gotoba feared the growing power of the new military government in Kamakura. He wanted to bring power back to the emperor and the traditional government in Kyoto. So in 1221 CE, he set in motion a chain of events that led to the embarrassing Jokyu war.

Gotoba assembled an army consisting of the Taira and other enemies of the Minamoto clan from the earlier Genpei War. Gotoba decided on the lines of succession for the throne without running it by the Kamakura government. He then held a festival, inviting all of his potential allies. He assumed those who refused were loyal to the Kamakura government over his Kyoto government. Gotoba even had one officer killed for exposing his loyalty to the shogunate.

A few days later, Gotoba declared the shogunate's regent, Hōjō Yoshitoki, to be an outlaw. The shogunate retaliated to this declaration by mobilizing their own army and heading for Kyoto. The Kamakura armies smashed their way through Gotoba's forces. Gotoba fled the city, seeking protection from the warrior monks of Mount Hiei. However, the monks could see the writing on the wall and refused to back the loser of this conflict. Gotoba's forces made one last stand at the bridge over the river Uji, the same site where the Genpei War began. The shogun army made short work of them and took the city of Kyoto for themselves. Gotoba and his sons were banished to the Oki Islands, never to return.

The Kamakura government began taking land from members of the losing side. The military government's power grew far greater than that of the traditional government.

# First Mongol Invasion

The next major battle would come as a threat from the mainland. The Mongols under the leadership of Kublai Khan had just made the Korean kingdom of Goryeo into a vassal state and were feeling optimistic about their chances of continued conquests. In 1266 CE and 1267 CE respectively, the Mongols had sent emissaries to Japan demanding they send tribute and agree to become a vassal state as well. Both times, Japan refused. Over the following years, the Mongols continued to send similar demands, but by this point, Japan wasn't even allowing the Mongol emissaries' ships to land.

The traditional Kyoto government thought it would be wise to try and negotiate with the Mongols rather than risk starting a war. But after the Shogunate had slapped all respect out of the Kyoto government in the Jokyu War, Kyoto's appeals fell on deaf ears. Instead, the proud Shogunate ordered all the landholders in Kyūshū, the province where the Mongols were most likely to attack, to return to their lands and prepare for battle.

In 1274 CE, the Mongols left the Korean Peninsula and landed on the Japanese island of Tsushima. The *jitodai* (deputy governor) along with his tiny force of 80 samurai rode out to meet the invading Mongol force of 8,000 warriors on 900 ships. The jitodai attempted to negotiate, but the Mongols promptly shot him dead with arrows and killed the 80 samurai. The Mongol forces then took the island of Iki with similar ease, defeating a resistance of 100 samurai. The Mongols allegedly hung the naked bodies of the women they murdered from the sides of their ships.

The Mongols reached Hakata Bay on November 19th. The Japanese defenders equaled them in number, but the Mongol battle tactics took the Japanese by surprise. The Mongols formed a phalanx using shields and poleaxes. They came equipped with bombs that spooked the Japanese horses and terrified the men.

The battle lasted a day and a half. The Mongol forces killed one-third of the Japanese defenders, forced them to retreat to Mizuki castle, and burned Hakata to the ground. The Japanese forces regrouped at Mizuki castle and made ready for a last stand against the terrifying invaders. But no such attack came. Legend says that a sudden typhoon arose that forced the

Mongol ships away from the island.

## Second Mongol Invasion

After the first invasion, the shogunate correctly guessed that the Mongols would try to invade again and began preparing for just such an event. In the years that followed, they constructed forts and walls at likely landing spots.

Kublai Khan sent even more emissaries to Japan to demand once again that Japan agree to become a vassal state and send tributes. This time they refused to leave without a response. So the Japanese cut their heads off and sent those back to Kublai Khan as a response.

The Mongols had just conquered the Song dynasty in China, meaning they had extra manpower for this second invasion. Kublai

Khan wasn't messing around this time, even using death row prisoners to bolster the size of his army. By the time he launched his attack in 1281 CE, he had 900 ships from Korea and 1,500 ships from southern China set to demolish all Japanese resistance.

This time, Kublai Khan had decided on a two-pronged attack strategy. A portion of the Mongol forces attacked from an Eastern Route heading again for the island of Tsushima then to Iki. They were supposed to wait for the Southern Route forces at Iki, but the commanders ignored their orders and went off to attack the Japanese mainland all by themselves. Not only that, but the Eastern fleet weakened themselves even further by splitting up Scooby-Doo style to invade both the Nagato Province and Hakata Bay simultaneously. The Japanese at Nagato pushed the Mongol forces back to Iki.

The forces that landed at Hakata Bay could not make it through all the fortifications the Japanese had put in place. The Mongols retreated to the islands of Noko and Shika with the Japanese launching a series of counter-attacks against them the whole while.

When the Southern fleet was finally able to meet up with the Eastern fleet, they tried to use their combined forces to Hakata, but again the Japanese held strong. Unable to land, the invading Mongol forces dropped anchor and fastened their ships together. Then, a powerful typhoon arose and completely demolished the invaders' ships. This typhoon would go down in history as *kamikaze* or divine wind. Even retreating ships were not spared. Mongol forces were seen in the water, clinging to pieces of their broken ships. When they washed ashore, they were executed by the Japanese. The Chinese, however, were spared since the Japanese felt they had only taken part in the attacks due to

Kublai Khan's coercion.

## Aftermath of the Invasion

While Japan's victory against the Mongol army was impressive, it caused some serious issues for the Kamakura government. Since this was a defensive war, Japan had acquired no new land. The government was running short on land to pay the samurai who fought off the invasion. Also, the Buddhist monks who had performed rituals and ceremonies to ward off the invaders were also demanding payment—declaring that their work had brought the *kamikaze*. Having fought valiantly and received little to no reward, dissent began to spread amongst the samurai class. Loyalty to the Kamakura government began to weaken.

As the samurai divided their land to give to their children, each successive generation had less land and resources than the previous one. The

Shogunate was aware of this growing unrest. To try to help the situation, the Kamakura government declared that samurai's land could only be passed down to one male heir. In the Heian era, land had been passed down to daughters which had given women more power. While mothers could pass on land to their daughters under this new policy, the number of landowning women began to taper off dramatically.

Another factor chipping away at women's rights in this era was the spread of Buddhism. The type of Buddhism that entered Japan had come through China. This meant it picked up Confucian ideas like the impurity of women. While Buddhism had existed in Japan during the Heian Period, it had then been practiced primarily by the upper classes. Now, in the Kamakura Period, Buddhism became prevalent in the provinces and amongst the commoners.

The three most common types of Buddhism in Japan at this time were Pure Land, Nichiren, and Zen Buddhism. Pure Land Buddhism appealed to commoners as it promised a way to reach the Pure Land, a type of Buddhist paradise. This sect centered around the worship of the Amida Buddha, such as repeating his name. Nichiren Buddhism, named for the priest who founded the sect, taught that enlightenment could be attained by reciting the Lotus Sutra. Finally, Zen Buddhism focused on knowing the true self by quieting the mind and acting spontaneously at the moment. The Zen sect was popular amongst the samurai class.

The Kamakura Period came to an end in 1333 CE under Emperor Go-Daigo as the result of a civil war called the Genkō Incident. Go-Daigo had been plotting to overthrow the Kamakura government, but they discovered his plans. The

Shogunate exiled Go-Daigo to Oki in 1331 (the same place Gotoba had been exiled). However, Go-Daigo was able to escape. General Ashikaga Takauji had been sent to defeat Go-Daigo and his men, but again the samurai class was becoming less and less loyal to the Kamakura government. Takauji sided with Go-Daigo and together they overtook Kamakura. Hōjō Takatoki and his entire family committed seppuku, ending the Hōjō clan's reign.

# CHAPTER 5
## *MUROMACHI PERIOD*

$T$he Muromachi Period, otherwise known as the Ashikaga Period, lasted from roughly 1333 - 1573 CE. Different sources will cite slightly different start and end dates to this period as we will see. For example, 1333 CE marks the date when the Kamakura government was overthrown in the Genkō Incident. Emperor Go-Daigo had begun this rebellion to bring power back to the Imperial court. After 148 years of military rule, Go-Daigo was thrilled by the success of his revolution. He immediately instituted the Kenmu Restoration, a move to completely restore the imperial court to its former glory. He failed, however, to secure the support of the samurai, such as the very ones who had helped him overthrow the Kamakura government in the first place. So in practice, the Kenmu Restoration amounted to little more than Go-Daigo's fantasy wish-fulfillment that was over almost before it started.

Ashikaga Takauji, the general who had defected from the Kamakura Shogunate to help Go-Daigo overthrow them, became the shogun himself. He established a new shogunate in 1336 CE. This new military government was set up in Ashikaga, just outside of Kyoto, and was thus called the Ashikaga Shogunate. Whereas the Kamakura Shogunate had operated alongside the traditional imperial court, the new Ashikaga Shogunate claimed all the authoritarian power for itself.

The time from 1336-1392 CE was known as the *Nanboku-chō* or Era of the Southern and Northern Courts. Whereas the Northern Court referred to the imperial court of the Ashikaga Shogunate, the Southern Court referred to the traditional imperial court of Go-Daigo. While it was clear that the military might rest with the Northern Court, the Emperor and his Southern Court were not entirely irrelevant. After all, the Emperor had the Imperial Regalia (otherwise known as the Three Treasures), which we discussed in Chapter 2: Mythology. These artifacts are a reminder of the divine authority of the emperor and how the spiritual significance of these tales was still firmly embedded in the nation's identity. It's easy to overlook the spiritual significance of this when viewed through a modern, scientific-materialist lens, but the traditional imperial government was still an influential entity.

# The Samurai

While we mentioned Japan's legendary warrior class in the previous chapter, the influence of the samurai would continue to grow and shape Japan. The samurai would leave a legacy that endures to this day. Much has been made of *Bushido,* the samurai code of conduct, and some of the most famous samurai conquests in Japanese history. Let's take a moment to examine just who the samurai were and how they came to leave their mark on the nation's history.

Prior to 792 CE, Japan had a national military. This was not a standing army, but rather a militia. Militiamen lived their normal lives as farmers until some threat to Japan occurred, and they were called to take up arms and defend the country. This was cheaper than maintaining a standing army because they were only used if they were needed. Any able-bodied men between the ages of 20 and 59 could be drafted as needed. In practice, each man served one month per year on average. Since they served so infrequently, they were not highly trained. Nobles from wealthy families that had access to horses and military training might become horseback archers.

In 792 CE, Emperor Kanmu ended the national military. The threat of Chinese invaders was slim since they were embroiled in their own conflicts elsewhere. And there were problems with the existing military model of Japan. There was little loyalty amongst the troops. People dodged the draft or deserted frequently. Governors were using the militia for non-military purposes, such as farming and other projects at the imperial government's expense.

The government started to place more emphasis on those with military training, such as the aforementioned horse archers. They created new titles and took to paying these specialized soldiers for hire whenever the need arose. So it was that in the 800s, a new class of warriors emerged in Japan.

Since social status and rank were closely tied to family lines, there were few opportunities for social mobility for those born outside of a high-ranking clan. The warrior class was appealing to those who had the means to acquire horses and armor but lacked the family name needed to ascend to the upper echelons of the imperial court. Now, however, the opportunity emerged to ascend the social ladder through heroism in battle. Titles, land, and favors were awarded to distinguished warriors. This new class or warrior was known as *bushi* or *samurai* (literally "one who serves").

There were many opportunities for samurai to

sell their services. Since more and more people owned private lands, there was a greater need to hire people to protect that land. They could also find work assisting in tax collection, fighting bandits, and quashing rebellions. They could be hired as bodyguards for nobles or even as police in cities.

Some samurai saw the benefit of banding together and forming gangs. The leaders, or warlords, were able to attract new members through promises of riches and other personal gains. These gangs could also form alliances with one another when it was mutually beneficial. This was the path that both the Taira and Minamoto clans we mentioned in the previous chapter used to advance their power and influence. They amassed armies in the provinces and sought favor by taking positions supporting high-ranking nobles in the capital.

While it seems that the growing military power of the warrior class could have posed a threat to imperial power, that wasn't the case—at first. During the Heian Period, samurai groups competed for the titles and acknowledgment of the more powerful clans of the imperial court. If a samurai acted against the ruling class, the court would label it as an act of treason. They would then bestow titles and power upon other samurai and send them to kill the offender, as in the case of Taira no Masakado attacking a provincial headquarters.

As we saw earlier, this all changed at the end of the Heian Period and the beginning of the Kamakura Period when the Minamoto clan rose to power during the Genpei War and established the Kamakura Shogunate. Now in the Muromachi Period, a new Muromachi Shogunate also made use of the samurai class. So in this period, we see a continued increase in the importance of the warrior class.

It's important to understand that the samurai were not loyal to some fuzzy idea of the Japanese state. Rather, they fought for personal gain. Their loyalty was to their clans and to their warlords. One way samurai were incentivized to be brave in battle was through the practice of head taking.

## Head Taking

The practice of removing and displaying the heads of one's enemies has ancient roots. It can be traced back at least as far as 200 BCE in China. Like much of Japanese culture, head taking was probably also imported from China. The earliest confirmed reports of head taking in Japan date back to the 900s CE. Though it cannot be confirmed, it is certainly plausible this could have begun even earlier.

The title of samurai was seen (usually) as an honorable position. In battle, it was common for one samurai to single out another on the battlefield and fight one-on-one. The victor would cut off the head of the loser, then present it to his lord for payment. This was a way for the samurai to prove their service in battle. Through this system, a samurai who had collected many heads would gain prestige and honor. In turn, taking the head of such a samurai would also bestow great honor.

One famous early example of head taking in Japan is the tale of Taira no Masakado. He was a Heian-era samurai who led a small rebellion in 939 CE in the provinces, capturing the local governor. In response, the imperial government in Kyoto put a price on Masakado's head. Roughly two months later in 940 CE, he was killed in battle. His head was brought back to Kyoto where it was displayed for the imperial court. The head was later brought to a small fishing village that would later become known as Tokyo. Masakado's head was buried there in a *kubizuka*, a type of grave. Masakado's head became deified and locals began to pay their respects at his *kubizuka*. At times, when his *kubizuka* was neglected, natural disasters seemed to befall Japan. Accordingly, his *kubizuka* is kept well maintained to this day. It is located in Tokyo's financial district on some of the most expensive real estate worldwide.

Prior to the Genpei War and the start of the Kamakura Shogunate, lords lacked the ability to promote samurai to higher social status and give them land to rule. After the war, the military-ruled the country, and *shugo* (military governors) had the power to give land and titles to the samurai. And the quickest way to advance in this new era of social mobility for the warrior class was to present to their lords the heads of the most prestigious enemy samurai they could acquire. The act of presenting these taken heads became a ceremony in itself, known as the "head viewing ceremony." It's important to note that even peasants could participate in these ceremonies. So if a feudal serf managed to collect the head of an enemy samurai and present it during a head viewing ceremony, he could be elevated to the status of samurai himself.

During a head viewing ceremony, heads had to be presented in an elegant and respectful manner. As such, a samurai preparing for battle would ensure his own head was presentable in case it should be cut off that day. However, it was ultimately the responsibility of the samurai to take the head to ensure the presentability of whatever heads he acquired. They would wash the head, comb its hair, and blacken its teeth to indicate its noble status. They would then wrap the head in a white cloth and place it on a wooden display, bearing the name of the samurai the head once belonged to as well as who took it.

There were, of course, some issues with this system. Some samurai would try to pass off a lowly footsoldier's head like that of a high-ranking samurai in order to receive a greater reward. Also, some samurai would leave the battlefield after they had collected an especially valuable head to ensure they got their reward before they were killed (one could say they were quitting while they were *ahead*). Also, removing heads could take a long time. In the heat of battle, when swiftness could mean the difference between victory and defeat, samurai would stop after each kill to see through the necks of each of their fallen foes. Even for all these drawbacks, the practice of head taking would continue in Japan up until WWII.

### Samurai Swords

The image of the samurai is all but inseparable

from their most iconic weapon—the sword. It is therefore important to take a look into the development and impact of the samurai sword in warrior culture and Japanese culture as a whole.

The *chokuto* (meaning "straight sword") or *tsurugi* was the earliest type of sword produced in Japan. These swords were roughly two feet long and were worn from the warrior's waist. This type of sword existed before the samurai. The technology to produce this type of sword most likely came from China. *Kusanagi no Tsurugi*, the sword of the Imperial Regalia, is this type of sword. These swords fell out of use around 900 CE.

The *warabite-to* was Japan's first curved sword. This style of the sword began to appear around 300 CE. The *warabite-to* was generally less than two feet long. In early versions, the sword had a straight blade with a curved handle. Over time, the sword evolved to become thinner. At the same time, a gentle curve was introduced to the blade.

The *tachi* (or "great sword") along with its smaller counterpart, the *kodachi*, were developed in the 900s CE. The *tachi* was longer than their predecessors at around 30 inches. In this sword, the entire blade is curved. Some scholars hypothesize that the move towards curved blades was to make the blade faster to unsheath and more useful for slashing, especially when wielded from on horseback (*All Types of Japanese Swords (history and how they were used)*, 2020). Another likely reason, however, was due to the introduction of a new process known as "differential hardening." This process made the swords more flexible and less prone to breaking. It also naturally resulted in the curvature of the blade.

During the Muromachi Period, the *uchigatana* (meaning "striking sword") became popular. This sword was less expensive than the *tachi,* making it popular with lower-ranking footsoldiers. These were worn with the blade facing up, allowing the user to draw the sword and strike in one single motion.

Also, during the Muromachi Period, the *katana* (meaning "single blade sword") appeared. This is the sword most commonly associated with the samurai today. It was around two to three feet long and was less curved than the *uchigatana.* Like the *uchigatana,* the *katana* was worn with the blade facing up, giving it the same benefits of unsheathing and slashing in one motion. While there is a common misconception that the *katana* was a samurai's primary weapon, this is not the case. Weapons, such as the bow and arrow or polearm, were preferred for their greater range. The *katana* was used as a last resort if a samurai was thrown from their horse or if they were fighting indoors.

Another sword of note is the *odachi* (literally "great big sword"), which was a single-bladed sword longer than three feet. It was briefly popular in the late Kamakura Period. This sword was used by samurai on horseback. Due to its length, it had to be worn on the swordsman's back making it difficult to unsheath. Because of its unwieldiness and impracticality, the *odachi* would fall out of use during the Edo Period.

## Warring States

Let's return now to our timeline in the Muromachi Period. As we stated at the beginning of this chapter, the new Ashikaga Shogunate had wrested control from Emperor Go-Daigo and the Imperial court. The powerful samurai class was composed of men motivated by personal gain over loyalty to their country. And Japan was on the verge of entering an era of near-constant war. This era was known as the *Sengoku Jidai* or the Warring States period. This was the golden age of the samurai.

In 1464 CE, shogun Ashikaga Yoshimasa had no heir. Therefore, there was no clear successor to replace him at the end of his time as a shogun. To attempt to avoid a potential dispute, he adopted his younger brother Ashikaga Yoshimi. This, he thought, would make for a smooth and peaceful transition of power at the end of his reign. But then, in 1465 CE, Yoshimasa had a son. This surprised Yoshimasa and threw a wrench into his plans of a smooth transition. Yoshimasa's wife, Hino Tomiko, obviously wanted their son to become the next shogun. Yoshimi and his supporters were none too pleased with this development. The debate became heated. This disagreement over who should be the next shogun erupted into armed fighting in 1467 CE in what would become known as the Ōnin War.

The central authority of Japan began to crumble. Daimyo ("regional warlords") scrambled to claim whatever lands they could in the ensuing chaos. Japan lost any semblance of national unity and became an island of roughly 100 warring fiefdoms that would battle for nearly 100 years.

In the Mikawa Province in 1548 CE, the mighty Oda clan invaded the Matsudaira territory. The Matsudaira turned to their nearest neighbor, the Imigawa clan, for help defending their land. The Imigawa agreed to lend their aid, provided their leader, Matsudaira Hirotada, sent his son, Matsudaira Motoyasu, for them to keep as a hostage. Lacking alternatives, Hirotada agreed. However, while Motoyasu was being transported to Imigawa territory, the Oda intercepted him and captured Motoyasu.

The Oda sent a missive to the Matsudaira with the ultimatum to either end their alliance with the Imigawa or they would kill Motoyasu. In a bold move, Hirotada writes back to Oda that they should kill his son if they must. That would only show the Imigawa how strong their alliance truly was. The Oda had not bargained on this. They decided to simply keep Motoyasu alive as a hostage until they could find some use for him.

During a siege by the Imigawa on the Oda clan, they offered to let the head of the Oda clan live if they agreed to hand over the castle they were attacking as well as Motoyasu. The Oda agreed. The Matsudaira leader had just recently passed, making Motoyasu the de facto head of the Matsudaira clan. The Imigawa saw this as a way of further strengthening their alliance with the

Matsudaira clan.

When Motoyasu reaches adulthood, the Imigawa return him to the Matsudaira clan. Under his leadership, the Matsudaira along with the Imigawa plowed through the Oda land. Motivated by the success of their campaign, the allied clans set their sights on Kyoto.

## *Oda Nobunaga*

The Oda were nearly defeated. They holed up in a castle prepared for one final stand. Their leader, Oda Nobunaga, gathered roughly 2,500 men to ride out against the roughly 25,000 Imigawa gathered before the castle. Nobunaga sends 500 of his men to create a diversion, pretending all his forces are gathered at a hilltop fort. The remaining 2,000 men launch an ambush on the distracted Imigawa army and slaughter them.

The Matsudaira who had been camping in a separate but nearby area witnessed the slaughter of the mighty Imigawa army at the hands of only a couple thousand Oda warriors. Impressed by this victory against all odds, Motoyasu (who would take the name Tokugawa Ieyasu) went to meet with Nobunaga and the two formed an alliance.

While the other clans to the east were embroiled in conflict amongst themselves, Nobunaga's new alliance with the Matsudaira (later renamed the Tokugawa) provided him a buffer and allowed him to move his troops towards, Kyoto without fear of enemy clans from the east invading Oda territory. Only two clans now stood between Nobunaga and Kyoto: the Azai and the Saito. To secure peace relations with the Azai, Nobunaga married his sister to the Azai's daimyo. Nobunaga also reaches out to his father-in-law, Dosan, who is the daimyo of the Saito clan. But before Dosan was able to formally establish peace between the Saito and Oda clans, he was killed in yet another dispute over succession called the Battle of Nagara-gawa. His successor, Saito Yoshitatsu, rejects any attempt at peace between the Saito and Oda clans.

At this point, it's important to briefly introduce another legendary samurai and daimyo: Toyotomi Hideyoshi. He began life as a lowly peasant before he got his first break as sandal-bearer to Oda Nobunaga. He gained Nobunaga's favor and got promoted to a higher position overseeing castle repairs. Keep an eye out for him, because he played a major role in the events to come.

### *Inabayama Castle*

Back to our timeline, from 1561-1563 CE the

Oda and Saito were locked in a fierce battle. The Saito remained deeply entrenched and managed to keep the Oda at bay. Nobunaga enlists the help of Hideyoshi. By this point, Hideyoshi had proven himself to be skilled in diplomacy. He approached Saito leaders and encouraged them one by one to defect to Oda's side. With this massive loss of support, the Saito was severely weakened but still held firm in their mighty fortress of Inabayama Castle. Nobunaga ordered Hideyoshi to construct a fortress for the Oda right at the foot of Inabayama Castle. Hideyoshi was able to construct this fortress too quickly for the Saito to launch an attack against it.

Hideyoshi had learned of a secret path through the mountains that would allow a small number of Oda men to sneak into Inabayama Castle undetected. Undercover of darkness, Hideyoshi and a small group of men successfully snuck into the castle and set fire to the storehouses and armory. The gunpowder in the armory exploded. Then Hideyoshi and his men threw open the gate to the castle, allowing Nobunaga and the rest of the troops to rush in and storm the castle. With the fall of Inabayama Castle, the Saito was defeated. Nobunaga granted Hideyoshi the title of daimyo for his valor and service. The end of the Saito meant the Oda had a clear path to march into Kyoto. The only thing Nobunaga lacked was a moral justification for invading. To invade without a valid reason would risk uniting the other clans against him. He would also risk losing his existing supporters.

### *Taking Kyoto*

The solution to this dilemma came in 1568 CE when Ashikaga Yoshiaki approached Nobunaga. He claimed he was the rightful heir to the office of the shogun. He asked for the support of the Oda to restore him to his proper station. Nobunaga leaped at the opportunity. He publicly declared that he was marching on Kyoto and that anyone standing against him was in defiance of the true shogun of Japan.

The Oda forces had little trouble securing Kyoto and making Yoshiaki shogun. However, Nobunaga had no intention of actually handing over control of Japan to Yoshiaki. Nobunaga made Yoshiaki send invitations to the nearby daimyo to come to a feast in Kyoto. Yoshiaki secretly sent letters to the daimyo stating Nobunaga was a traitor and calling for them to take him out. This, obviously, seemed suspicious to the daimyo. When many of them, such as the Asakura, refused to attend the feast, Nobunaga declared them to be traitors and declared war against them. To reach the Asakura, Nobunaga had to march his troops through Azai territory. Nobunaga assumed this would go smoothly since he had secured their allegiance through marrying his sister to the Azai clan leader. When Nobunaga reached the

Azai territory, however, the Azai switched sides to join up with the Asakura clan. Nobunaga was able to split his army and escape, but he vowed vengeance against the treacherous Azai. During their escape, a ninja assassin named Hachisuka Tenzō fired two shots at Nobunaga before slipping off into the woods. The attack was unsuccessful as both bullets lodged in Nobunaga's armor.

In July of 1570 CE, the Oda and Tokugawa forces marched into Azai territory. They approached the Azai's main castles along the Anegawa River, where they were met by the combined Azai and Asakura forces. While the Oda and Tokugawa forces were victorious, the battle left the Oda too weakened to continue their advance, so they retreated to Kyoto. Recognizing how much the Oda forces were weakened, the Miyoshi clan whom the Oda had kicked out of Kyoto saw their chance at revenge. The Miyoshi forged an alliance with a band of militant, Buddhist warrior monks known as the Ikko-Ikki from the temple of Ishiyama Hongan-ji.

## *Warrior Monks*

The Ishiyama Hongan-ji temple, which lay just south of Kyoto, had been a thorn in Nobunaga's side for some time. The monks had refused to pay taxes, disrupted trade, and were a major obstacle in Nobunaga conquering Japan. So Nobunaga, along with 30,000 men, went to surround Ishiyama Hongan-ji temple. When the Oda forces attempted to advance, the muddy marshland slowed their progress. The 3,000 monks armed with arquebuses (an early version of the musket) prevented Nobunaga's troops from advancing further. Unable to take the temple, but also unwilling to admit defeat, Nobunaga's forces camped around the temple for the next 11 years. This became the longest siege in Japan's history.

While all this was going on, the Asakura and Azai allied with another group of warrior monks from Enryaku-ji, a temple on Mount Hiei. Unable to have enemies on all sides, Nobunaga makes a truce with the Asakura and Azai clans. Learning from the 11-year siege at Ishiyama Hongan-ji, Nobunaga decides to demolish the Enryaku-ji temple by setting the forest around it on fire and ordering his troops to kill anyone who tried to flee.

## *Ieyasu's Most Successful Loss*

By 1571 CE, Nobunaga had launched even more campaigns against warrior-monk temples. He was able to use his growing military strength to crush the Azai and Asakura clans. Meanwhile, Shogun Ashikaga Yoshiaki was still pleading for someone to help him take back control from Nobunaga. Answering the call was one of the most famous samurai of the Sengoku Jidai:

Takeda Shingen. He planned his own march on Kyoto through Mikawa, Tokugawa Ieyasu's home province. Ieyasu assembled troops to stop Shingen in Mikawa. Ieyasu made the mistake of setting up his arquebusiers on an open plain, leaving them susceptible to Shingen's signature military maneuver: the cavalry charged. The cavalry demolished Ieyasu's forces.

By the time Ieyasu made it back to his castle stronghold, he had only five men remaining. What Ieyasu did next could be considered an act of madness, genius, or perhaps a mixture of the two. He had his men (just five men, remember) light all the lamps along the castle walls. Then, Ieyasu's men opened the castle gates and began to beat drums. Shingen's men were understandably confused. This appeared to them to be some kind of trap. So Shingen's men waited outside the castle. When night fell, Ieyasu sent the now-famous ninja, Hattori Hanzo, and his ninja comrades to attack the

Takeda troops and cause confusion. This attack led Shingen and his forces to believe Ieyasu was hiding a great number of men in the castle, so the Takeda retreated.

## Nagashino Castle

In 1573 CE, Takeda Shingen once again set his sights on Kyoto and rode with his troops into Mikawa. However, a sniper shot and killed Shingen in battle. Shingen's less adept son, Takeda Katsuyori, took his place. Under Katsuyori, the Takeda attacked Nagashino castle. The Takeda invaders greatly outnumbered the Mikawa defenders and pushed them back into the castle's keep. One of the defenders, a man called Suneemon, volunteered to sneak past the Takeda lines and come back with reinforcements. Suneemon was able to reach Ieyasu and Nobunaga and tell them about the siege. Nobunaga and Ieyasu agreed to come to their aid. Suneemon decided to ride ahead to inform the besieged Mikawa that help was on the way, but the Takeda captured him before he could make it back.

Takeda Katsuyori told Suneemon that he would spare his life if Suneemon agreed to shout to the castle that no help was coming. Suneemon agreed. The following day, the Takeda brought Suneemon out in front of the castle tied to a crucifix. When it came time for him to call out to the castle, he yelled that Nobunaga and Ieyasu were on their way. The Takeda killed Suneemon with spears, but the defenders received his message. Their morale boosted by Suneemon's news, they held the castle. When Ieyasu and Nobunaga's troops arrived, they completely demolished the Takeda forces.

The Takeda forces that did remain, made an alliance with the Uesugi clan and the warrior monks of Ishiyama Hongan-ji. Uesugi Kenshin was considered by his clan to be a living embodiment of the kami of war. However, in 1578 CE, while preparing an invasion of Oda land, Kenshin died of esophageal cancer. With the Uesugi weakened by the loss of their powerful leader, Nobunaga was able to finally defeat the warrior monks of Ishiyama Hongan-ji and what remained of the Takeda clan.

Nobunaga and Ieyasu were touring the Kansai region when they received a request from Hideyoshi for reinforcements for a siege. Nobunaga sent his general Akechi Mitsuhide to lead an army to assist Hideyoshi, while he himself went through Kyoto first to attend to some business there. Nobunaga spent the night in the Honno-ji temple. Mitsuhide marched his army through Kyoto. When they came to Honno-ji temple, Mitsuhide turned traitor. He ordered his men to attack the temple. They massacred Nobunaga's men. Nobunaga retreated to the inner sanctuary, lit it on fire, and committed seppuku rather than being captured.

This left Ieyasu in a precarious situation. He was now in the Kansai region with just a small number of men and the treacherous Mitsuhide army between him and the Tokugawa territory hundred of miles to the east. Fortunately, Ieyasu had the legendary ninja Hattori Hanzo with him. Hanzo was able to show Ieyasu a secret path to sneak around the Mitsuhide forces and finally make his way back to Tokugawa territory.

Mitsuhide, now in control of Kyoto, began to kill anyone he thought posed a threat to his newly stolen power, starting with Nobunaga's family. Hideyoshi got wind of Mitsuhide's betrayal and rode with his army back to Kyoto to crush Mitsuhide's troops. Mitsuhide was killed after officially holding the title of shogun for just three days. The local daimyo met and agreed on an heir to the shogun, the then two-year-old Oda

Hidenobu. This allowed Hideyoshi to become regent and to be the real influence behind the office of the shogun.

Tokugawa Ieyasu agreed to acknowledge Hideyoshi as his lord. In exchange, Hideyoshi granted the Tokugawa special privileges. Importantly, the Tokugawa were exempt from serving in Hideyoshi's army for the next decade.

Hideyoshi held a vision of unified Japan, so he implemented three major reforms. This included revising the tax structure; stripping all peasants of their swords and guns and outlawing them from owning any in the future, and finally establishing a rigid caste system and forbidding anyone from rising up from the caste they were born into. Hideyoshi also instituted a policy that peasants were tied to the land they lived on and could not travel freely. These policies so stabilized Japan that they remained in place more or less unchanged until 1871 CE.

The only remaining issue Hideyoshi faced was what to do about the samurai class. These were, after all, armed warriors whose only profession was killing. So to occupy the samurai, Hideyoshi sent them on a campaign with the insanely ambitious goal of conquering China. The campaign never got further than Korea. Japan had to end the fighting and retreat after losing hundreds of thousands of men with nothing to show for it. The one group of warriors that was spared was the Tokugawa clan. Remember, Hideyoshi had granted them a 10-year exemption from military service.

## *The End of the Sengoku Jidai*

In 1598 CE, Regent Toyotomi Hideyoshi died of an unknown illness. Shortly before his death, he had assembled a group of five feudal lords known as the Council of Five Elders to act as regents for his five-year-old son. Among them was none other than Tokugawa Ieyasu.

Many lords were bitter over the failed Korean campaign and wanted the power to pass to a Tokugawa. Others were afraid of the growing Tokugawa power. Still, some schemed to exploit the fact that a child was a shogun and steal power for themselves.

A former administrator under the late Hideyoshi, a man named Ishida Mitsunari, was one such man who had his eye on the prize of ultimate power. He plotted to assassinate Ieyasu. He also tried to make it seem as though the Maeda clan were co-conspirators in his plot. However, Ieyasu learned of the plot and informed the Maeda. The Maeda pledged their loyalty to Ieyasu and planned to kill Mitsunari. Mitsunari went to Ieyasu to beg for mercy, which Ieyasu granted. However, Mitsunari continued scheming about how he could claim power. He forged an alliance with a mutual enemy of the Tokugawa, the Uesugi.

In 1600 CE, the Uesugi marched into Tokugawa territory under the leadership of Uesugi Kenshin's heir, Uesugi Kagekatsu. Ieyasu's ally, Torii Mototada, held a castle that would almost certainly be one of the first places the enemy attacked as it was between them and Kyoto. Mototada pledged to hold his castle against the invaders knowing full well that he would die in the process. Mototada and his 2,000 men held the castle for 10 days against an invading force of 40,000 strong. Before the castle fell, the Torii had taken a chunk out of the Ishida forces. The 10-day delay allowed Ieyasu to rally his troops and repel the Uesugi.

Then the Ishida and the Tokugawa met at Sekigahara. The forces were evenly matched, neither side had a clear advantage. A division of 16,000 men on the Ishida side under the command of Kobayakawa Hideaki had stayed out of the battle on a hilltop, simply watching. All at once, they rushed down from the mountain and betrayed the Ishida by smashing into their flank, turning the tide of the battle. The Ishida were quickly defeated and the Ieyasu's forces won.

The Emperor granted Ieyasu the title of shogun in 1603 CE. He ruled for just two years before retiring and passing the title of shogun to his son, Tokugawa Hidetada. At this point, Hidetada was an adult who had already proven himself in battle. Because Hidetada was actually a competent leader and his father, the great Ieyasu, was still alive, his authority as shogun went unchallenged.

The only remaining potential threat to

Tokugawa power was Toyotomi Hideyori, Hideyoshi's son. Hideyori remained secure in Osaka castle until, in 1614 CE, the Tokugawa decided to attack it and eliminate this one final threat. Osaka castle fell the following year, finally ending the Sengoku Jidai.

# CHAPTER 6
## *EDO AND MEIJI PERIODS*

The Edo Period lasted from 1603 to 1867 CE. This time, following the turbulent Sengoku Jidai, was characterized by peace and isolation from the rest of the world. When Tokugawa Ieyasu had finally become shogun, he established the shogunate capital in Edo. He had distributed land amongst the daimyo in a way that would prevent any of them from growing too powerful; he would take land from daimyo who displeased him and give it to daimyo who had earned his favor. He mandated these daimyos spend every other year in Edo, further ensuring their loyalty to the shogunate. The success of these reforms is evident in the 250-year reign of the Tokugawa shogunate and the stability of this era.

## Life in Edo Japan

A political system known as *bakuhan* emerged. Under this system, the shogun held all authority on a national level while the daimyo held authority on the local level. The daimyo was connected to the shogunate through an increasingly complex bureaucracy. The dominant philosophy of the age was Confucianism, which extolled values such as loyalty and hard work that helped support the rigid caste system Ieyasu had implemented. The social hierarchy went as follows. The emperor was at the top of the social order, though as we've already seen any real power the emperor had was long gone. Below that was the shogun who held all real authority. Beneath the shogun was the daimyo. Under that were the samurai, who were still praised for the valor they had displayed during the Sengoku Jidai but had little chance for heroics in this era of stability and peace. Beneath that were artists, merchants, and peasants.

While the capital still officially remained in Kyoto where the emperor resided, Edo (modern-day Tokyo) was the most important and powerful city in Japan. Given Tokyo's size today, it may be surprising to consider what small and unassuming village Edo was when Tokugawa Ieyasu selected this location for shogunate headquarters in 1603 CE. Since he required all the daimyo to have a second home in Edo. The shogun also stipulated that the daimyo had to leave their wives and children in Edo when they returned to their home provinces. Since Edo became a meeting point for the wealthy elites, artisans and merchants also flooded to the city as they realized the business potential that existed there. The city would grow from just a few thousand residents to become the largest city on Earth by 1721 CE when the population was estimated at around one million. Many public bathhouses (*sentō*) were built to accommodate the burgeoning population. These became important social centers much as their counterparts in ancient Rome had been.

The dense concentration of wooden houses made Edo prone to the many fires it experienced, notably the Great fire of Meireki in 1657 CE. According to legend, this fire began when a priest attempted to burn a cursed kimono. The three previous owners had all died before they had been able to wear it. When the priest set fire to the kimono, a gust of wind spread the flames. Before anything could be done to stop it, nearby buildings caught fire. This ensuing conflagration destroyed roughly two-thirds of the city and claimed 100,000 lives. In the aftermath, the government instituted new safety standards and reorganized the city to prevent any recurrence of such a tragedy.

Like in the prior Heian Period, this era of peace allowed people to appreciate the natural beauty of Japan. Cherry blossoming viewing (*hanami*) and moon viewing (*otsukimi*) became popular pastimes for people of all social classes. The merchant class did especially well during this time. They were flush with cash from the growing wealth of Edo. At the same time, they weren't held to the same moral standards as the samurai or daimyo classes. They enjoyed lavish, hedonistic lifestyles in the city's growing pleasure districts. There was a proliferation of erotic artwork set in these brothel districts known as *ukiyo-e*, literally "floating world art." The "floating world" referred to the lifestyle of seeking transient worldly pleasures. During the Edo Period, the technique of woodblock printing (*mokuhanga*) allowed for works of art to be mass-produced, driving down the price and making art more accessible than ever before. One very famous example from the late Edo Period is the iconic woodblock print called *The Great Wave off Kanagawa*, a work by Hokusai as part of his ambitious project *Thirty-six Views of Mount Fuji*. Kabuki theater also began during the Edo Period and was popular entertainment for the lower and merchant classes.

The Tokugawa shogunate initially supported trade with foreign nations but was wary of foreigners and foreign ideas. Ieyasu had sought to make the ports of Edo the main port for foreign traders, but Europeans opted to use ports in Kyushu instead. This posed a threat to the authority of the Edo government. At the same time, Daimyo in and around Kyushu began to convert to Christianity, a foreign ideology that posed a threat to the caste system. After finally achieving stability and control, the Tokugawa shogunate was not about to let foreigners destabilize the country once again. By 1616 CE, Christianity was forbidden. And finally, the Closed Country Edict of 1635 CE was implemented. This strict order forbade Japanese people from leaving the country and any who had left from returning. In 1637 CE, overtaxed peasants and unhappy Christians took up arms in what would be known as the Shimabara Rebellion. A large number of unhappy samurai came to aid the rebels and fought so tenaciously that the 100,000 Japanese men sent by the shogun were unable to quash the rebellion. Finally, the shogun was able to enlist the help of the Dutch East India Company who supplied the weapons. They were finally able to quash the rebellion. For their help, The Netherlands got the exclusive right to be the only western country Japan traded with for the next two and a half centuries. Likely experiencing flashbacks from the Sengoku Jidai, the Tokugawa shogunate aggressively closed its borders to the dangerous and destabilizing foreigners.

This ushered in a period of extreme isolation known as *sakoku* ("locked country") that lasted for over 250 years. The policy of Japanese isolationism would last until it was brought to an end in 1853 CE by U.S. Commodore Matthew C. Perry.

## Commodore Perry Opens Japan

If anyone was qualified for the difficult task of opening Japan to foreign trade, it was Commodore Matthew C. Perry. Born in Rhode Island, USA in 1794 CE, Perry had a decorated naval career. He had served aboard the *USS Cyane* in 1820 CE, carrying freed Black slaves to help establish the country of Liberia. He patrolled African waters to suppress pirates and slave traders. He was an avid proponent of naval education and the then-novel technology of steam-powered ships, earning him the moniker "The Father of the Steam Navy." He had negotiations with the top admiral of the Turkish Navy, the kingdom of Naples, the President of Liberia, African chiefs, Mexican tribal leaders, and the British Navy. Tsar Nicholas I of Russia was so impressed with Perry, he offered him a position as an admiral in the Russian Navy.

Prior to 1852 CE, Japanese policy against foreign ships landing in Japan was so extreme that even shipwreck survivors who washed ashore would be imprisoned or even executed. This provided America some justification for forcing a trade agreement with Japan. It's also worth noting that America was in the era of Manifest Destiny, where they were growing and expanding with virtually no end in sight. They had also profited tremendously from the opium trade with China. This had led to the Opium

Wars, which showcased the military might of western powers and would have rightly given Japan cause for alarm.

In 1852 CE, US President Millard Fillmore assigned Perry the task of persuading Japan to agree to safely return shipwrecked American sailors, allowing U.S. ships to dock in Japan to take on coal and water, and most importantly opening Japan to foreign trade. President Fillmore gave Perry complete authority to secure the best terms with Japan he could.

In 1853 CE, he arrived with the first steam-powered ships the Japanese had ever seen. The Japanese referred to these as *kurofune* ("black ships"). The Japanese Navy surrounded these boats and ordered Perry and his men to leave. Perry refused to leave until he was allowed to deliver a letter from President Fillmore to Emperor Kōmei. Claiming he was celebrating the U.S. Independence Day, Perry had all his ships fire off blanks and explosive cannonballs. The Japanese, feeling now that negotiation was necessary to their survival, ultimately allowed Perry to land in Kurihama on July 14, 1853. Having delivered the letter, Perry promised he would return for a reply the following year.

Perry returned in 1854 CE with an even larger naval force. When he landed on March 8th, Perry made a point to make the greatest show of it he could. He sent three bands to march ahead of him in formation playing the Star-Spangled Banner. Perry himself marched outflanked by two of the largest African-American sailors in his squadron, a completely novel sight in *sakoku* era Japan. When negotiations began, the Japanese delegates agreed to allow U.S. ships to land at two specific ports to take on coal and water. They also agreed to return the imprisoned U.S. sailors. But they did not yet agree to open trade relations with America.

At this point, the U.S. and Japanese exchanged gifts with one another. Perry had come prepared with some gifts intended to tantalize Japan into considering what wonders they could expect if they opened trade with the U.S. Perry gave gifts of modern revolvers, rifles, two telegraph sets, and Perry's *pièce de résistance*, a fully functional ¼ scale railroad and engine. To celebrate the signing of the treaty, both sides gave great feasts with large quantities of food and alcohol. One story goes that one of the intoxicated Japanese commissioners came up to Perry and threw his arm around Perry's neck and ruined Perry's epaulets. He told Perry through an interpreter "Japan and America. All the same heart." One of Perry's men asked why Perry had tolerated this. Perry reportedly replied, "Oh, if they will only sign the treaty, he may kiss me" (Morison, 1967).

On March 31, 1854, both the U.S. and Japan signed the Treaty of Kanagawa. But the U.S. wasn't satisfied that they hadn't secured trading rights with Japan, so in 1858 CE another U.S. envoy named Townsend Harris negotiated just such an agreement with the Harris Treaty. This effectively ended Japan's period of isolation. This ushered in an era when an unindustrialized Japan was strong-armed into a series of unequal treaties with the industrialized West.

## Meiji Restoration

While the Edo Period had been an era of peace, it had also been a pressure cooker with tensions boiling just beneath the surface. All the strict policies the Tokugawa shogunate implemented served to maintain the status quo within Japan for centuries. They had also managed to deal with foreign policy by sticking their fingers in their ears and ignoring how the rest of the world had been modernizing. But now the West had shown up at their doorsteps with warships and weapons and buffaloed their way in. Within Japan, there was growing unrest as well. Virtually all of the wealth and cultural benefits we described in the previous section were limited to Edo. In the provinces, peasants were forced to remain on their land incurring heavy taxes and famine while the samurai class enjoyed leisure time and wrote poetry. The samurai looked on as the merchant class that was supposedly beneath them in status lived lavish lifestyles and partied in brothels.

As we stated previously, the Dutch were the one western nation that Japan traded with during the period of isolation. *Rangaku* ("Dutch studies") served as the sole link between Japan and Western knowledge during this time. Intellectuals became fascinated with these new and innovative ideas, especially in the fields of science and technology. This would help form the foundation for the rapid technological advancement to come.

Now the daimyo watched as the supposedly powerful shogun kowtowed to western power and signed unequal treaties left and right. Their loyalty began to wane. Realizing the need to modernize if they wanted to survive, Shogun Tokugawa Iemochi opened schools to study Western thought and technology. At the same time, what could be described as a nationalist, an anti-Western terrorist group called the *shishi* ("men of great purpose") began to form in the southern province of Choshu with the rallying cry *sonnō jōi* ("revere the emperor, expel the barbarians"). They began to assassinate westerners and fire on western ships attempting to land in Japanese harbors. In 1864 CE, the *shishi* even tried to take Kyoto. They were unsuccessful, but the writing was on the wall. The absolute control the Tokugawa shogunate had wielded was rapidly beginning to crumble. The *shishi* soon realized that Western influence was here to stay whether they liked it or not. So they adopted the new motto: *wakon yōsai* ("Japanese spirit, western technology").

Meanwhile, U.K. Diplomat Sir Harry Parkes consulted with Japanese samurai and diplomat Saigō Takamori to discuss how British weapons and tactics could be used to rebel against the shogunate. In 1866 CE, Tokugawa Iemochi died and was succeeded by a new shogun, Tokugawa Yoshinobu. The following year, Emperor Kōmei died of an unknown illness and was succeeded by then 14-year-old Emperor Meiji.

With this swift political restructuring, the pro-imperial (anti-shogunate) clans of the Satsuma and the Chōshū formed an alliance known as the Satchō Alliance with the stated purpose of killing Shogun Yoshinobu and restoring the power of the emperor. When Yoshinobu discovered this, he offered to step down to take a position beneath the emperor as the head of the council. The Satchō Alliance refused and called for him to completely renounce all political power. So in 1868 CE, Yoshinobu stepped down declaring a full restoration of all imperial power.

However, Yoshinobu wasn't content to give up without a fight. He rallied the daimyo who were still loyal to him and went to war in an event known as the Boshin War. On January 27, 1868, the shogunate forces attacked Kyoto. While the Imperial forces were outnumbered, they had the benefit of modern weapons (such as rifles, Gatling guns, and howitzers), and were able to repel the attackers. Some of the daimyo loyal to the shogun began to defect after seeing the power of these modern weapons. By May of that year, the Satchō Alliance had reclaimed Edo and forced the former shogun to surrender. Yoshinobu was stripped of his land and titles and put under house arrest. Even so, a coalition of clans to the north refused to surrender to imperial rule. Once again, the imperial arsenal of modern weapons allowed them to crush the last of the anti-imperialist resistance by October of that year. The imperial court was moved to the thriving metropolis of Edo, which was renamed Tokyo ("eastern capital"). The last vestiges of the resistance retreated to Hokkaido and were defeated five months later. This "restoring" of power to the emperor is the reason this era is often called the Meiji Restoration, though, in truth, it was the first time all of Japan truly had a single centralized government.

Now that this power dispute was settled, Japan had an even bigger task on its hands. The protracted period of isolation had left the country centuries behind the industrialized West. In order to be relevant on the world stage, Japan had to do in decades what had taken the West centuries. They quickly implemented public education, discarded the caste system in favor of social mobility, and replaced the samurai with a conscription army which all able-bodied men had to serve for 3 years. The new focus for Japan would be national pride instead of a feudal hierarchy.

The samurai were not pleased to be stripped of their rank. Saigō Takamori's home province of Satsuma became a hotbed of discontent. When a plot by the Imperial government to assassinate Takamori was discovered, an armed group left for Kyoto to demand an explanation. The following battles would be known as the Satsuma Rebellion. In 1877 CE, while on the way to Kyoto, they encountered Kumamoto Castle and their advance was halted. They laid siege to the castle but were eventually repelled by the new conscript army. The samurai were driven back to Kagoshima, where they made their final stand at the Battle of Shiroyama. The new conscript army outnumbered the samurai 60-

to-1. Takamori and his men fought until the last man fell dead, ending in a final suicide charge of just 40 samurai against the mighty conscription army. Takamori would be remembered as a tragic hero and the last great samurai warrior. Putting down this rebellion was so costly to the Imperial government that they were forced to abandon the gold standard.

Meanwhile, Japan was rapidly industrializing. Massive public works projects were underway putting in railways and telephone infrastructure. The emperor hired consultants from across Europe to guide Japan in this period of rapid modernization. Women were still held as inferior to men and expected to hold their "traditional" roles as wives, mothers, and housekeepers. But everyone, including women, was given four years of public education. This enabled the nation to standardize the Japanese language across the country and help promote national identity through a common curriculum. Public schools were also able to incorporate an expanded version of the Bushido code to promote the virtues of honor and service.

The western influence could also be seen in art. New western-inspired art that focused on realism was called yōga ("western-style paintings") as distinct from nihonga ("Japanese-style paintings"). Western styles of architecture were incorporated into Japan's growing cities as well. In 1889 CE, the ban on playing cards was lifted which allowed a company called Nintendo (yes, *that* Nintendo) to begin producing them. In the midst of all this rapid change, there was a very real fear that Japan was losing its national identity. The one defining trait of the Japanese national identity that the people could rally around was the emperor. In 1889 CE, Japan adopted its first constitution. They set up a cabinet, prime minister, and bicameral legislature. But even these were seen as gifts from the emperor.

Even as Japan was incorporating advancements and technology from the west, they sought to assert their uniquely Japanese sense of identity. Japan used this as justification for expanding their empire by "liberating" other Asian countries from western control by conquering them. To this end, Japan annexed the Ryukyu Islands in 1879 CE. In 1894 CE, Japan overtook Korea. When China attempted to help liberate Korea from Japanese control, the newly modernized Japan easily repelled the Chinese forces. Japan then annexed Taiwan. In 1904 CE, Russia challenged Japan for control of Manchuria and Korea. Japan offered a compromise, but Russia refused. In the ensuing Russo-Japanese War, Japan demolished Russia in the first-ever victory of an Asian nation over a western power in modern times.

# CHAPTER 7
## *TAISHO PERIOD THROUGH WWII*

Emperor Meiji died in 1912 CE after 44

years as emperor. The throne was peacefully passed to Emperor Taishō, who was largely kept out of the public eye due to neurological ailments likely brought about by a childhood case of cerebral meningitis. Even so, the Japanese Empire continued to grow. At the end of the First World War, Japan was represented at the Treaty of Versailles though they were largely ignored. Britain and France claimed massive amounts of land for themselves, while the Japanese presented a racial equality clause to be included in the preamble to the new League of Nations. They hoped to secure for themselves an equal seat at the negotiation table. This clause was roundly rejected by the Council. This slight poured gasoline on the fire of Japan's anti-Western sentiment.

# Invading China

In 1932 CE, Japan invaded Manchuria before pushing forward into China. On September 27, 1940, Japan signed the Tripartite Pact with Italy and Germany and officially joined Germany and Italy to form the Axis Powers of World War II. The reasons Japan joined were varied. Most of the Allied Powers, especially the U.S., disapproved of Japan's conquest of China. Japan was still reeling from the exclusion of its equality clause from the League of Nations. It seemed obvious to Japan that the Allied Powers would never treat them as equals. Japan also felt war with the Western powers was inevitable and felt an alliance with Italy and Germany would help deter the U.S. from coming to China's aid. The other major threat to Japan's conquest of China was Russia.

Japan wanted Russia to join the Axis powers, but Germany refused, so instead Japan and Russia signed a nonaggression pact. Another reason Japan joined the Axis Powers was that Germany had just annexed the Netherlands and France. Japan feared that this would mean Germany would soon control the French Indo-China and the Dutch East Indies. Japan desperately needed resources from these regions. It is also worth noting that, at the time Japan signed the Tripartite Pact, it was perfectly reasonable to assume that Germany was going to win the war.

Japan used this opportunity to declare a region of control for themselves known as the Greater East Asia Co-Prosperity Sphere (GEACPS).

In 1940 CE, the U.S. placed an oil embargo on Japan to try and arrest their growing power. Japan retaliated by bombing several U.S. naval sites, most famously Pearl Harbor. This event prompted the U.S. to formally enter World War II.

## War Crimes

The Second World War was an extremely dark time for Japan. During this war, Japan committed unspeakable atrocities for which the Japanese government has still never taken full responsibility. In the final days of the war, Japan began burning documents concerning "comfort women." Between 1932 and 1945 CE, between 100,000 to 200,000 women and girls were trafficked into sex slavery. These women were sent to government-sanctioned "comfort stations," where they were beaten and raped, sometimes as often as 40 times per day by members of the Japanese military. When it became clear that the existing supply of sex workers in Japan would not be enough to satisfy the Japanese army, they began posting fake job advertisements for positions such as secretaries and nurses with the promise of high salaries. Women who applied for these jobs would instead be forced to become sex slaves. When this ruse was discovered, the government began paying gangs to supply them with women. The gangs would procure these women often by simply snatching them off the street (*Why Japan Got off Easy in WW2 - The HORRIBLE Atrocities of the Japanese Empire*, 2021).

Another black mark on Japanese history from this era comes from the doctors who worked for the Epidemic Prevention and Water Purification Department of the Kwantung Army, more commonly known as Unit 731. This group based in Northern China conducted depraved and nightmarish experiments on civilians and POWs. All of these experiments were officially sanctioned by Emperor Hirohito (later known as Emperor Showa). The stated purpose of these experiments was to learn how the human body responded to various diseases under various conditions. Almost all of the people used in their experiments were healthy individuals. Many were infected with diseases and then dissected while still alive. They forcibly impregnated women, so that they could see the effects of their experiments on mothers and their fetuses. The experimenter replaced living human blood with animal blood or seawater, burned or electrocuted them, used a centrifuge to spin them to death, along with a myriad of other bizarre and grotesque experiments.

One practical purpose of Unit 731 was to identify what pathogens could be used in biological warfare against the Allied Forces, specifically the United States. General Ishii was weeks away from implementing a plan to airdrop fleas infected with this pathogen over the U.S. when Japan surrendered.

At the end of the war, U.S. General MacArthur granted all those involved with Unit 731 a full pardon in exchange for their research. The research was later deemed to be too unscientific to be of any medical use.

## Nanjing Massacre

The Japanese also committed what was known as the Nanjing Massacre or the Rape of Nanking, a six-week period of slaughter and rape by the Japanese army beginning December 13, 1937. In the course of this event, the Japanese killed anywhere from 30,000 to 400,000 Chinese. This incident is one of the worst cases of mass rape in recorded history.

Many of those targeted by the Japanese soldiers were high school students. Contests were held to see who could cut off the most heads in a given amount of time. In some cases, women were literally raped to death.

Even today, the national war memorial to Japanese servicemen who died from 1868 to 1954 at Yasukuni Shrine displays the names of over 1,000 known war criminals out of the over 2 million names displayed. There is no acknowledgment of their crimes. Some 14 of these are class-A war criminals. Japan's crimes in WWII are still heavily propagandized to this day. Though most modern Japanese do acknowledge the atrocities, some far-right nationalist groups still deny them.

On August 6, 1945, the United States dropped the first atomic bomb on Hiroshima. The bomb killed between 70,000-80,000 people, around

50,000-60,000 of whom were civilians. Over 90% of doctors and nurses in Hiroshima were killed in the bombing. After the bombing, U.S. President Harry S. Truman announced, "If they do not now accept our terms, they may expect a rain of ruin from the air, the like of which has never been seen on this earth" (*Truman Statement on Hiroshima*, n.d.). Baron Kantarō Suzuki reiterated Japan's commitment to never surrender. Three days later, on August 9, 1945, the U.S. dropped a second atomic bomb on Nagasaki. The death toll estimates for the second bombing range between 39,000 to 80,000. On August 14, 1945, Emperor Hirohito officially surrendered.

# CHAPTER 8
## *POSTWAR PERIOD*

$A$t the end of the war, the most pressing

issue facing the Japanese people was starvation. The dissolution of the Japanese Empire meant Japan no longer had access to the foreign food supplies they had come to depend on. U.S. General MacArthur was tasked with disarming and democratizing Japan. MacArthur found it advantageous to keep Emperor Hirohito in place to keep the support of the Japanese people. At the Tokyo War Crime Trials of 1946, Prime Minister Hideki Tojo and other military leadership received most of the blame. Japan's military was disarmed and Shinto was removed as the state religion. Previously imprisoned political dissenters were freed and women were given the right to vote. Over a third of the farmland in Japan was purchased from large landlords and corporate entities that held it and were resold to farmers at low prices. This allowed millions of farmers to become landowners and the old feudal system of land ownership crumbled.

The U.S. Army also spearheaded the creation of a new constitution that guaranteed general elections, free speech, freedom of religion, the right to a fair trial, and womens' suffrage. The first free elections in Japan were held on April 10, 1946. Shigeru Yoshida became the first democratically elected prime minister of Japan. His policies focused on rebuilding Japan's lost infrastructure and on economic growth. At this time, Japan relied completely on the U.S.

military for protection against foreign threats. The money not spent on the military was used towards industrial expansion. Japan's economy received another massive boost as Japan supplied materials for the war.

# Economic Miracle and Burst Bubble

As a result of the improved infrastructure and new technology, the Japanese economy was transformed into a consumer economy. The government invested large sums into social welfare and education. As a result, the workforce became highly productive. Factories began to produce automobiles, steel, electronics, and tech. Japan gained a reputation for reliability and precision in its manufacturing. By the 1960s, Japanese goods were in high demand and the country found itself in a trade surplus, exporting more products than it was importing. The soaring economy that resulted was known as the Economic Miracle. In just two short decades, Japan had gone from a war-torn, occupied country in shambles to one of the most developed and prosperous countries in history. The U.S. even feared Japan would eclipse America's economy.

In the 1970s, Japan's economic growth slowed. An event known as the OPEC Oil Embargo hit hard, as Japan depended heavily on foreign oil. Even so, the economy still grew throughout the decade. By the 1980s, the country's per capita GDP was greater than that of the U.S. This growth begat speculation that led to a massive housing bubble.

By the 90s, the bubble finally burst. A recession ensued and the economy stagnated. With decreased purchasing power, consumers bought fewer goods which meant the price of goods had to increase since fewer were being sold. This further compounded the problem. The deflation that began in this period still affects Japan to this day.

Today, Japan has one of the oldest populations in the world. The country currently has a population of roughly 147 million, but due partially to a low birth rate this number is projected to fall below 100 million by 2049. This loss of population could mean an economic downturn is on the horizon for Japan, but if history shows us anything, it is the resilience of this nation. Through new technology and expanding opportunities for foreign workers wanting to enter the country, Japan will very likely find a way.

# CONCLUSION

Now finally, we have reached the end of our history of Japan. Let's take a moment to recap what we've learned.

We've examined Japan as it grew from its early origins as a hunter-gatherer society with the Jomon People. We've seen the Yayoi bring technology, such as metalworking from China, and start an elaborate network of permanent settlements. We learned the legends behind the

Imperial Regalia, or Three Treasures, that represent the divinity of Japan's emperor. We discovered the Nara period when the Fujiwara clan began their rise to power and Japanese writing became widespread. We saw how the peace of the Heian Period allowed for innovations in art such as the first-ever novel.

We studied the Genpei War, where Japan's first shogunate rose to power. We saw Japan repel not one, but two Mongol invasions. We learned about the samurai and saw them battle for 150 years during Japan's turbulent Warring States period. We learned of life under the peaceful, but a strict rule of the Tokugawa shogunate in the Edo Period. We saw Japan isolate itself from the rest of the world for roughly 250 years. Then, we watched as the country reopened trade and modernized at an unprecedented rate.

We saw the emperor return to power during the

Meiji Restoration, followed by an overflow of nationalism. We saw Japan join the Axis Powers and go down a dark chapter in her history. Then we saw how this led to the nation's postwar rebuild and created one of the largest economies in the modern-day.

This has been a complex journey, but we hope we have summarized it in a complete and interesting way. Whether you are a scholar or a history enthusiast, hopefully, you have been able to see the history of Japan in a new light. If there's one thing to take away from this book, it's that Japan's history is a story that deserves to be remembered.

# REFERENCES

Akatani, M. (2016). [The Cause of Death of Taira no Kiyomori: A Possible Connection with the Death of Fujiwara no Kunitsuna]. *Nihon Ishigaku Zasshi. [Journal of Japanese History of Medicine]*, 62(1), 3–15. https://pubmed.ncbi.nlm.nih.gov/27464420/.

*All Types of Japanese Swords (history and how they were used).* (2020, August 29). Www.youtube.com. https://www.youtube.com/watch?v=oT8m3AOV_IY.

Axelrod, J. (2019). *NPR Choice page.* Npr.org. https://www.npr.org/sections/codeswitch/2019/08/11/742293305/a-century-later-the-treaty-of-versailles-and-its-rejection-of-racial-equality.

*Commodore Perry and the Opening of Japan.* (2021, February 7). Www.youtube.com. https://www.youtube.com/watch?v=MaZ95O6RmAc.

*Emperor Go-Daigo.* (2020, June 9). Wikipedia. https://en.wikipedia.org/wiki/Emperor

_Go-Daigo.

Feature History. (2017). Feature History - Meiji Restoration. On YouTube. https://www.youtube.com/watch?v=Y_ b58Rpg2YY.

*History Summarized: The Meiji Restoration.* (2020, May 8). Www.youtube.com. https://www.youtube.com/watch?v=Y5 zlKYYp7bs.

How'd It Happen? History. (2017). What Happened to Japan after WW2? (How'd It Happen? History). In *YouTube.* https://www.youtube.com/watch?v=Lg 4tQOEqU3o.

https://www.facebook.com/thoughtcodotcom. (2019). *How to Be Beautiful in Heian Era Japan.* ThoughtCo. https://www.thoughtco.com/beauty-in-heian-japan-195557.

*Imperial Regalia of Japan.* (2020, April 26). Wikipedia. https://en.wikipedia.org/wiki/Imperial _Regalia_of_Japan.

*Izanagi.* (2020, November 8). Wikipedia. https://en.wikipedia.org/wiki/Izanagi

*Japan Omnibus - History - Early Japanese*

*History*. (2018). Japan-Zone.com. https://www.japan-zone.com/omnibus/history1.shtml.

*Japanese history: Postwar*. (2002, June 9). Japan-Guide.com. https://www.japan-guide.com/e/e2124.html.

*Japanese Mythology - Myth Encyclopedia - god, story, legend, names, ancient, tree, famous, animal, world, Chinese*. (2010). Mythencyclopedia.com. http://www.mythencyclopedia.com/Iz-Le/Japanese-Mythology.html.

Kiger, P. J. (2019, September 20). *10 Inventions From China's Han Dynasty That Changed the World*. HISTORY. https://www.history.com/news/han-dynasty-inventions.

*Life in Edo Japan (1603-1868)*. (2019, April 27). Www.youtube.com. https://www.youtube.com/watch?v=wI ygLo_W1Sw&t=456s.

Linfamy. (2019). Life of Early Japanese Women (So Much Cheating...) | History of Japan 38 [YouTube Video]. In *YouTube*. https://www.youtube.com/watch?v=Ylo m3pm5SCo.

*Minamoto no Yoritomo.* (2020, March 11).
    Wikipedia.
    https://en.wikipedia.org/wiki/Minamot
    o_no_Yoritomo.

*Mongol invasions of Japan.* (2020, June 4).
    Wikipedia.
    https://en.wikipedia.org/wiki/Mongol_
    invasions_of_Japan.

Morison, S. E. (1967). Old Bruin Commodore
    Matthew C .perry 1794-1858. In *Internet
    Archive.*
    https://archive.org/stream/in.ernet.dli.
    2015.130945/2015.130945.Old-Bruin-
    Commodore-Methew-C-perry-1794-
    1858_djvu.txt.

*Origins of the Yayoi people.* (2008, June 27).
    Heritage          of          Japan.
    https://heritageofjapan.wordpress.com/
    yayoi-era-yields-up-rice/who-were-the-
    yayoi-people/.

*Prehistory of Japan (Paleolithic, Jōmon and
    Yayoi          periods).*          (n.d.).
    Www.youtube.com. Retrieved November
    30,          2021,          from
    https://www.youtube.com/watch?v=8Q
    4fRT081-0.

Proctor, M. (2015, June 25). *Japanese*

*Mythology: 5 Ancient Myths and Legends.* TakeLessons Blog. https://takelessons.com/blog/japanese-mythology-z05.

Taika era reforms | Japanese history | Britannica. (2019). In *Encyclopædia Britannica.* https://www.britannica.com/event/Taik a-era-reforms.

*The Heian Period, an Age of Art...Ending in a Shogunate | History of Japan 34.* (n.d.). Www.youtube.com. Retrieved December 2, 2021, from https://www.youtube.com/watch?v=9z 8ZZezVmfw.

*The Jomon, a 10,000 Year Old Culture (and Pots!) | History of Japan 3.* (n.d.). Www.youtube.com. Retrieved November 30, 2021, from https://www.youtube.com/watch?v=gD BB5nazfM4.

*The Rise of Japan: How did Japan become one of the World's Largest Economies?* (2021, January 31). Www.youtube.com. https://www.youtube.com/watch?v=ytr pRLOaPzM

The Shogunate. (2019). The Samurai Tradition

of Taking Heads. On *YouTube.*
https://www.youtube.com/watch?v=TX
PrkZ5Kpmo.

*The Yayoi Arrive...and Change EVERYTHING!
| History of Japan 4.* (n.d.).
Www.youtube.com.
https://www.youtube.com/watch?v=bD
nV9UvrpaU&t=5s.

*Truman Statement on Hiroshima.* (n.d.).
Atomic Heritage Foundation.
https://www.atomicheritage.org/key-
documents/truman-statement-
hiroshima#:~:text=If%20they%20do%2
0not%20now.

*Volcanoes of Japan: facts & information /
VolcanoDiscovery.* (2020).
Volcanodiscovery.com.
https://www.volcanodiscovery.com/jap
an.html.

W, S. (2013, November 8). *The Ainu.* Tofugu.
https://www.tofugu.com/japan/ainu-
japan/

*Warring States Japan: Sengoku Jidai - Battle
of Okehazama - Extra History - #1.*
(2014, November 8). Www.youtube.com.
https://www.youtube.com/watch?v=hD
sdkoln59A&list=PLhyKYaoYJ_5A649vE

Qk37316BH8FsaU24.

*Warring States Japan: Sengoku Jidai - How Toyotomi Unified Japan - Extra History - #5.* (2015, January 17). Www.youtube.com. https://www.youtube.com/watch?v=lB D8OAegEwo&list=PLhyKYaoYJ_5A649 vEQk37316BH8FsaU24&index=5.

*Warring States Japan: Sengoku Jidai - The Campaign of Sekigahara - Extra History - #6.* (2015, January 31). Www.youtube.com. https://www.youtube.com/watch?v=5vs cOHPFUfo&list=PLhyKYaoYJ_5A649v EQk37316BH8FsaU24&index=6.

*Warring States Japan: Sengoku Jidai - The Death of Oda Nobunaga - Extra History - #4.* (2014, December 20). Www.youtube.com. https://www.youtube.com/watch?v=ht6 h4- MsMOY&list=PLhyKYaoYJ_5A649vEQ k37316BH8FsaU24&index=4.

*Warring States Japan: Sengoku Jidai - The Siege of Inabayama Castle - Extra History - #2.* (2014, November 22). Www.youtube.com.

https://www.youtube.com/watch?v=I2y
T2nitGDk&list=PLhyKYaoYJ_5A649vE
Qk37316BH8FsaU24&index=2.

*Warring States Japan: Sengoku Jidai -
Warrior Monks of Hongan-ji and Hiei -
Extra History - #3.* (2014, December 6).
Www.youtube.com.
https://www.youtube.com/watch?v=G3
frtoMaxZE&list=PLhyKYaoYJ_5A649v
EQk37316BH8FsaU24&index=3.

*Why Japan Got off Easy in WW2 - The
HORRIBLE Atrocities of the Japanese
Empire.* (2021, June 6).
Www.youtube.com.
http://youtube.com/watch?v=uBEmMe
ZOYaI.

Wikipedia Contributors. (2019a, March 12).
*Genpei War*. Wikipedia; Wikimedia
Foundation.
https://en.wikipedia.org/wiki/Genpei_
War.

Wikipedia Contributors. (2019b, July 3). *Nara
period*. Wikipedia; Wikimedia
Foundation.
https://en.wikipedia.org/wiki/Nara_per
iod.

Wikipedia Contributors. (2019c, September 14).

*Sengoku period*. Wikipedia; Wikimedia Foundation. https://en.wikipedia.org/wiki/Sengoku_period.

Wikipedia Contributors. (2021a, April 18). *Ōnin War*. Wikipedia; Wikimedia Foundation. https://en.wikipedia.org/wiki/%C5%8Cnin_War.

Wikipedia Contributors. (2021b, August 12). *Dōkyō*. Wikipedia; Wikimedia Foundation. https://en.wikipedia.org/wiki/D%C5%8Dky%C5%8D.

Wikipedia Contributors. (2021c, October 27). *Jōkyū War*. Wikipedia; Wikimedia Foundation. https://en.wikipedia.org/wiki/J%C5%8Dky%C5%AB_War.

WorldAtlas. (2019, January 18). *Why Is Volcanic Soil Fertile?* WorldAtlas. https://www.worldatlas.com/articles/why-is-volcanic-soil-fertile.html.

# OTHER BOOKS BY HISTORY BROUGHT ALIVE

- Ancient Egypt: Discover Fascinating History, Mythology, Gods, Goddesses, Pharaohs, Pyramids, and More from the Mysterious Ancient Egyptian Civilization.

Available now on Kindle, Paperback, Hardcover & Audio in all regions

- Greek Mythology: Explore The Timeless Tales Of Ancient Greece, The Myths, History & Legends of The Gods, Goddesses, Titans, Heroes, Monsters & More

Available now on Kindle, Paperback, Hardcover & Audio in all regions

- Mythology for Kids: Explore Timeless Tales, Characters, History, & Legendary Stories from Around the World. Norse, Celtic, Roman, Greek, Egypt & Many More

Available now on Kindle, Paperback, Hardcover & Audio in all regions

- Mythology of Mesopotamia: Fascinating Insights, Myths, Stories & History From The World's Most Ancient Civilization. Sumerian, Akkadian, Babylonian, Persian, Assyrian and More

Available now on Kindle, Paperback, Hardcover & Audio in all regions

- Norse Magic & Runes: A Guide To The Magic, Rituals, Spells & Meanings of Norse Magick, Mythology & Reading The Elder Futhark Runes

Available now on Kindle, Paperback, Hardcover & Audio in all regions

- Norse Mythology, Vikings, Magic & Runes: Stories, Legends & Timeless Tales From Norse & Viking Folklore + A Guide To The Rituals, Spells & Meanings of Norse Magick & The Elder Futhark Runes. (3 books in 1)

Available now on Kindle, Paperback, Hardcover & Audio in all regions

- Norse Mythology: Captivating Stories & Timeless Tales Of Norse Folklore. The

Myths, Sagas & Legends of The Gods, Immortals, Magical Creatures, Vikings & More

Available now on Kindle, Paperback, Hardcover & Audio in all regions

- Norse Mythology for Kids: Legendary Stories, Quests & Timeless Tales from Norse Folklore. The Myths, Sagas & Epics of the Gods, Immortals, Magic Creatures, Vikings & More

Available now on Kindle, Paperback, Hardcover & Audio in all regions

- Roman Empire: Rise & The Fall. Explore The History, Mythology, Legends, Epic Battles & Lives Of The Emperors, Legions, Heroes, Gladiators & More

Available now on Kindle, Paperback, Hardcover & Audio in all regions

- The Vikings: Who Were The Vikings? Enter The Viking Age & Discover The Facts, Sagas, Norse Mythology, Legends, Battles & More

Available now on Kindle, Paperback, Hardcover & Audio in all regions

# FREE BONUS FROM HBA: EBOOK BUNDLE

Greetings!

First of all, thank you for reading our books. As fellow passionate readers of History and Mythology, we aim to create the very best books for our readers.

Now, we invite you to join our VIP list. As a welcome gift, we offer the History & Mythology Ebook Bundle below for free. Plus you can be the first to receive new books and exclusives!

Scan the QR code to join.

## Keep up to date with us on:

YouTube: History Brought Alive

Facebook: History Brought Alive

www.historybroughtalive.com

Printed in Great Britain
by Amazon